The Early Jesus Movement and Its Parties

The Early Jesus Movement and Its Parties

A New Way to Look at the New Testament

Harry W. Eberts Jr.
Paul R. Eberts

YBK Publishers
New York

YBK Publishers, Inc.
39 Crosby Street
New York, NY 10013
www.ybkpublishers.com

The Early Jesus Movement and Its Parties:
A New Way to Look at the New Testament

ISBN 978-0-9824-012-3-1

Library of Congress Control Number: 2009937283

Manufactured in the United States of America
or in the United Kingdom when distributed elsewhere

09-11

Table of Contents

Preface and Acknowledgments

Harry and Paul Eberts, brothers, both graduated from Wheeling High School, Wheeling, West Virginia; from Heidelberg College, Tiffin, Ohio; and from Yale University Divinity School, New Haven, Connecticut.

Paul went from Yale to the University of Michigan in Ann Arbor and completed his Ph.D. in sociology, working especially with Dr. Gerhard Lenski; Paul did some of the research for the groundbreaking study titled *The Religious Factor.* He taught at the State University of New York in Binghamton, then went to Cornell University, where he stayed until his retirement in 2007. His field of study at Cornell was rural sociology—which later changed its name to development sociology; he worked frequently with the Legislative Commission on Rural Resources of New York State government. Among his many publications is *Well-Being Indicators for New York State, 1950–2000* (Albany: Legislative Commission on Rural Resources, 2004), the latest of the studies he undertook every ten years that marked changes in census-based socioeconomic trends in the state's counties. Based in the land-grant part of Cornell University, he also worked extensively with county extension agents, traveling at one time or another to every county in the state for presentations, and was the first director of Cornell's Community and Rural Development Institute. Through CaRDI, he helped train more than one hundred students from the United States and all over the world in community and rural development theory and methods. Through extension, his research on and presentations in the counties became well-known for emphasizing what county people can do to improve their life-quality.

Harry, the older brother, became a minister of the Presbyterian Church, USA, and served parishes in Ohio, California, and Illinois. Always interested in serving the community through the parish, he pioneered in day care for children, retirement homes for the elderly, ecumenical relations among churches, and in helping to integrate public school systems. Always interested in continuing education for ministry, he received his degree of Doctor of the Science of Religion (STD) from San Francisco Theological Seminary in San Anselmo, California. In 1978, Harry and his wife were invited to Egypt to talk about reformed theology to members of the Coptic Evangelical Church in Egypt. Carrying on this work, they returned to Egypt nine times, teaching and preaching, observing Egyptian life, learning from the Egyptians of their two millenia of Christian faith and practice (important in many ways to this study), and preparing ministers of the churches in Egypt for graduate work in the United States. Harry's book *We Believe: A Study of the Book of Confessions for Church Officers* (Philadelphia: Geneva Press, 1987) grew out of his work in local churches with which he ministered in the Presbyterian Church (USA) as well as with presbyteries with which he was affiliated throughout the United States.

It was natural for these two brothers to be drawn to a sociological study of the early Christian movement. Both became interested in Christian ethics, and studied at Yale with H. Richard Niebuhr whose groundbreaking studies *The Social Sources of Denominationalism* (Hamden, CT: Shoestring Press, 1954, orig. 1929), *The Meaning of Revelation* (New York: Macmillan, 1941), and *Christ and Culture* (New York: Harper, 1951), especially, gave interpretations of Christianity from a social-science perspective.

Many other studies have been undertaken concerning the impact that Christianity made upon the social systems it confronted and the impact of those social systems upon the faith. Among these are Wayne Meeks' two works, *The*

First Urban Christians (New Haven and London: Yale University Press, 1983) and *The Moral World of the First Christians* (Philadelphia: Westminster Press, 1986), as well as Rodney Stark's *The Rise of Christianity* (Princeton, NJ: The Princeton University Press, 1996) and Adolf von Harnack's *The Acts of the Apostles* (London: Williams & Norgate, 1909). We are especially indebted to these works.

Another kind of scholarship began to emerge that located individual communities in the early Christian movement. Gerd Thiessen, *Sociology of Early Palestinian Christianity* (Philadelphia: Fortress Press, 1977) described the impact of the Christian movement on rural Palestine and decided that it had made little headway there. Robert Brown, *The Community of the Beloved Disciple* (NewYork: Ramsey; Toronto: Paulist Press, 1979) began to write about a community gathered around the Beloved Disciple and to see it as a distinctive form of the early Christian movement. He was preceded in his work by Oscar Cullmann, *The Johannine Circle* (Philadelphia: Westminster, 1976) who saw a circle of influence gathering around the Beloved Disciple; R. Alan Culpepper, *The Johannine School* (Missoula, MT: Scholars Press, 1975), who called this a "school" with the Beloved Disciple at the center; and by C. H. Dodd, a scholar whose groundbreaking work, *Historical Tradition in the Fourth Gospel* (Cambridge, U.K.: Cambridge University Press, 1963) may have been the father of these works. Walter Schmithals in *The Office of Apostle in the Early Church* (New York and Nashville: Abingdon, 1969) was among the first to challenge Acts' assertion that "the Apostles were the disciples after the resurrection" and to identify the Apostles as a distinctive movement within the early church.

In addition, Howard Kee's two works, *Community of the New Age* (Philadelphia: Westminster, 1977) and *Who Are the People of God? Early Christian Models of Community* (New Haven and London: Yale University Press, 1995) looked beyond the above to multiple forms of early Christian community; he identified at least seven such communities, some of them reflected in the four Gospels themselves. F. F. Bruce, *Peter,*

Stephen, James, and John (Grand Rapids, MI: Eerdmanns, 1979) actually named the persons that we identified in our studies but did not see them in terms of leaders of parties within the Jesus movement, such as we were able to identify, especially through a careful reading of Luke's *The Acts of the Apostles* combined with Paul's Letters.

Largely in contrast to previous writings, the starting point in our study was with the creed of the early church found in 1st Corinthians 15. This creed identifies three leaders and three parties as carrying on Jesus' mission: Peter and the Twelve, James and the Brethren, and Paul and the Apostles. To these three we add a fourth, one that was out of favor at the moment the creed was formulated in a conference in Jerusalem. This was the party of Stephen, Philip, and the Christian Hellenists (culturally Hellenist converts to Judaism)

Owing to the difficulties Greek-speaking gentile converts had in conforming to the dietary, marriage, and especially circumcision laws followed by members of the Hebrew-speaking synagogues, the other three parties (that is, excluding the Hellenists) had come together in a conference in Jerusalem. There they generated a compromise, namely, that the parties could admit men to their congregations without their being circumcised but, once admitted, all persons in the church were to abide by the historic marriage and food laws practiced by Hebrew-speaking, Torah-observant Jews.

But even this compromise did not satisfy Greek-speaking gentile converts. Much of the divisiveness among the parties was due to unwillingness by these converts to live up to the compromise. These differences also kept the four parties in the early Jesus movement in enough disarray that overall unity became impossible. This theme is major in cutting across the four chapters that examine the parties in turn.

From these starting points, in reading through the New Testament we could identify other relative differences among the four parties as well—in their beginnings, ethnic compositions, forms of governance, mission fields, worship practices, theologies, and ethics. The chapters on each party spell out these differences. On such issues the parties often competed with one another even as they often cooperated in carrying out their respective missions. These four chapters are preceded by a brief history of the beginning of the Jesus movement in Judea and Galilee and are followed by a concluding chapter of reflections on the movement and its parties.

We invite readers, then, to become acquainted with what we consider the inner dynamics of these four most important parties in the earliest Jesus movement: the Disciples, the Brethren, the Hellenists, and the Apostles. Their dynamics reflect major issues that have carried over throughout the entire Christian era.

Harry and Paul Eberts, November 1, 2009

CHAPTER 1

Introduction

The Parties and their Characteristics

From birth to death Jesus of Nazareth was confronted with certain realities he had to take into account in his ministry.

One was the brooding power of the Roman Empire. Rome's legions ruled from the south of Egypt and the northern boundary of the Sahara desert in Africa to the Danube River in central Europe, to the mountains bordering the Slavic nations to the east and to what is now England's border with Scotland in the British Isles. No earlier "western" nation had ever ruled this much territory.

The Jews were one of the favored ethnic groups in the empire. They were permitted to celebrate their Sabbath, to try matters in their own courts, and to use some of their taxes to support their religious practices, even the temple in Jerusalem where they made their sacrifices. This was the benevolent face of the Roman Empire. But on great Jewish feast days, the Romans were likely to parade their power. Their banners and soldiers were on every street corner. Jesus' friends and neighbors faced exorbitant taxation that could lead to expropriation of lands and slavery for themselves and their families. Roman couriers could impress any Jewish man, no matter what he was doing, to carry his load for exactly one mile. Jesus used this custom as a parable to his people: *"...if someone compels you to carry his burden one mile, carry it two"* (Mt 5:41).

In addition to Roman power, the Palestinian Jewish community was subject to the family of the Herods. These rulers, who were not Jews but Idumeans, served as Rome's surrogates in the two provinces of Galilee and Judea. Their kings were supported by a clan-like party called the Herodians. This party supported the Herodian dynasty, did its best to keep the dynasty in power, and embraced without question any practice the Herods advocated.

The Herods' rule, like the power of their Roman masters, was far from benevolent. Herod, called the Great by his devotees, killed members of his own family because he thought they were plotting against him. People were indiscriminately arrested, tortured, and executed. Often their families did not know what had happened to them, or why or how; they were what in our time have come to be called "the disappeared." Under these conditions, pressure for rebellion began to press upon Jerusalem.

In life and in death, Jesus lived under the weight of the Roman Empire and its surrogates. A course of taxation that took place around the time of the birth and early childhood of Jesus caused an insurrection in Galilee. According to reports, Herod put it down by summarily executing some 3,000 men, about 600 of them by crucifixion. The situation in Judea was even worse. Brigands and terrorists, some called *lestes* and others *sicarii*, roamed the land and as often as they could struck down Roman officials and Jews they saw as collaborators. Unrest in Judea was so great that Tiberias, the Roman emperor in those years, had to appoint a prefect in the place of the Herod who was ruling, and so Pontius Pilate came on the scene about 26 C.E. Eventually, Rome identified Jesus as one of its rebels and crucified him.

In addition to the governments of Caesar and Herod, Jesus was confronted with a number of parties within Judaism itself.

One such party was the Sadducees. The Sadducees were the party of wealthy priests and their aristocratic friends. As such they combined conservative religious attitudes with power politics. Their center of strength was the temple, but their main interest lay in protecting the status quo and maintaining their own political power. They extensively collaborated with the Romans and adapted to certain Roman cultural influences like the theater and the race track. In effect, they "played ball" with the Romans, figuring they would be there when the Romans were gone, and they would still have their temple, sacrifices, position, and wealth. In crises, rather than trying to protect the Jewish people, they tended to close their eyes to everything the Romans were doing, including terrorizing people, to control insurrectionist tendencies.

Almost opposite to both the Sadducees and Herodians were the Pharisees. They were a party that tried to maintain the Jewish Law, the Torah, and traditions that they themselves had added to the Law. They ate only kosher foods, refused to eat with those who did not strictly keep the Law, and scrupulously observed the Sabbath. They refused to touch anyone who was ill and thought that any gentile, or woman, was "unclean." They tried to apply the same laws to lay people that priests applied to themselves. In effect, their prayer was, "Thank God I am not a gentile; thank God I am not a slave; thank God I am not a woman." The result of their position was that they did not want to have any contact with the world around them—slaves, gentiles, Romans, women, children. In politics and religion, they were pacifists because any sort of physical combat would bring them into contact with blood and gore and all kinds of unclean things.

Even more concerned with removing themselves from contact with the world were the Essenes. These men (they seem to have been nearly all men; few skeletons of women have been found in the cemetery of their base at Qumran) formed a community in the Judean desert adjacent to the Dead Sea. The caves and buildings in which they lived and worked were secluded, remote from the busy life of Judea and Galilee. There they ate, slept, lived, and died, worked on their manuscripts and dreamed of the coming battle when God would vindicate his faithful. In fact when the battle came, a Roman legion marched down the Dead Sea's shores and attacked Qumran; the community hid its manuscripts, died in the slaughter, and disappeared from history. It was only about sixty years ago (in the late 1940s) that archeologists discovered their caves, began to recover their manuscripts, and reclaimed their work's history.

Another set of Jews, more a movement than a group, were the precursors to the Zealots. In the New Testament these men were variously called thieves, robbers, and bandits– *lestes,* in Greek. while *zaelotes* (zealots) was the name the movement widely assumed when armed revolt broke out around 65 C.E. This revolt led to a siege of Jerusalem and the destruction of the temple. These men were the terrorists of their day with a program of obtaining weapons, a dagger or sword, and driving the Romans out. They moved stealthily, stole what they needed to live, food and clothing alike, and attacked Romans, Herodians, and Sadducees where they could. They generally caused such havoc in Galilee and Judea that the emperor had to remove the family of Herod from rule in Judea and Jerusalem and make personal appointments from Roman citizens like Pontius Pilate to quell insurrectionist tendencies.

Especially vicious in this movement were the assassins called *Sicarii,* named for the short-bladed sharp knives they carried under their flowing garments to strike at Roman officials or Jewish collaborators when the opportunity arose. Scholars have puzzled over the name "Iscariot" that was attached to Jesus' follower Judas. Possibly Iscariot is an Aramaicized form of *sicarii,* so that the real title for Judas was "Judas the Knife." In what is now Palestine, bandits and assassins were at work during Jesus' time to a degree that we are just beginning to understand today.

Along with many conformist individuals and groups, and slaves and serfs, the above parties were the types of movements that had already emerged in the midst of the turmoil and chaos when the Jesus movement came onto the scene.

In contrast to the alternatives formulated by these groups, Jesus began his ministry with the proclamation, *"The time is fulfilled and the kingdom of God is at hand. Repent, and believe the gospel* (Mark 1:15). These words stand as a frontispiece for the Gospel of Mark certainly, and in essence for the whole New Testament. This proclamation sums up the message Jesus came to bring. Everything he said and everything he did expressed these sentiments.

The beginning of the Jesus movement was hardly conducive to popular success. Jesus had preached and ministered in Judea for about three years and in Galilee for a few months when he determined to go to Jerusalem to confront the authorities. In the confrontation he was crucified and his followers scattered. But some among his followers were convinced that God had raised him from the dead—"resurrected" was the term they used—and they gathered together to continue the ministry of healing, teaching, and preaching that Jesus had begun. They were convinced that in his resurrected body he would continue to give them guidance, support, comfort, and love. They started out courageously.

They chose a man named Matthias as the successor of the deceased Judas. In doing this, they restored the Disciples to their Jesus-chosen number. At Pentecost, approximately fifty days after Jesus' crucifixion, Peter preached to a gathering of Jews who had come from diaspora cities to gather in the city of Jerusalem. Three thousand, according to Acts (2:41) were baptized that day and became part of the fellowship. Acts offers this idyllic picture of them, *"Day by day, attending the temple together and breaking bread in their homes, they partook of food with glad and generous hearts, praising God and having favor with all the people. And the Lord added to their number day by day those who were being saved"* (2:46–47).

The Disciples continued their preaching and healing, and large numbers of people were added to their fellowship (4:4, 5:12–16). Arrested frequently and consigned to jails, they emerged just as frequently and continued their work of preaching and healing.

Then catastrophe came. Hebrew-speaking Jewish Christians rose up against Greek-speaking Hellenist Christians. The contending parties were both parts of the Jesus movement, but they differed measurably from each other in their faith and practices. For the Hebrew party the temple was the center of their faith, and they went there regularly to sacrifice and pray. They met in synagogues where Hebrew was spoken and Hebrew Scriptures were read. They retained as much of historical Jewish life as possible. The Hellenists, while also coming from a Jewish background, met in synagogues where Greek was the language of teaching and prayer, and Scriptures were read from the Septuagint, the official Greek translation of the Hebrew Scriptures.

In addition, "Hellenist" and "Hebrew" represented two different ways of life. Hebrews were more strict in applying their food laws and in marrying Hebrew husbands and wives. Hellenists were more lax in these matters. So the Hellenist branch set itself up as a distinct and separate part of the Jesus movement. Its overall leadership was given to "The Seven," mostly Christians with Greek-sounding names, with one called Stephen foremost among them.

In the first utterance credited to him in Acts, Stephen the Hellenist made an incendiary speech in the presence of Hebrews. He said that the temple was an apostate institution and that the Law honored and observed by Hebrews was not directly from God (Acts 7:44–53). Predictably, these words upset the Hebrew group, so much so that *"they were enraged and ground their teeth at Stephen"* (Acts 7:53). And indeed they seized and killed him. In Stephen's death the Jesus movement had its first martyr.

Stephen's death marked a turning point in the life of this early Jesus movement. Its unity was destroyed. Now two groups, not one, made up the movement, and they were soon joined by two others. The roster came to read like this: Peter and the Twelve; Philip and the Hellenists; James, the brother of Jesus, and his Hebrew-speaking Brethren; Paul and the Apostles. Each group conducted its mission in different arenas: Peter among Galileans and along the Gaza strip; Philip with Hellenist Jews in the wider Mediterranean world; James going to Hebrew synagogues wherever he found them inside and outside Jerusalem; and Paul approaching the larger gentile world.

From his headquarters in Jerusalem, James, who was known from the beginning of the movement as "the brother of Jesus," observed that Peter and Paul seemed to be pushing the envelope of faith and practice. Paul, working in gentile cities of Galatia, had begun to baptize persons into the faith who were not yet circumcised, and he insisted that the spirit of Jesus led him to do it. In Caesarea, Peter had a vision that convinced him that gentiles should be accepted into the faith without observing the food laws and without circumcision (Acts 10:24–29). In Antioch, Peter ate with gentiles. But when emissaries came to Antioch from James in Jerusalem, Peter drew back, separating himself from those who had adopted Paul's way (Gal 2:11–12). James, noting these actions, summoned the two to Jerusalem to work out the issues before them.

The most prominent parties represented in the Jerusalem conference were "the Twelve and Peter," "the elders and James" (representatives of the Brethren), and "Paul and the Apostles." The Hellenists were not represented. At the gathering, Peter told what had happened in Caesarea when he met and ate with a Roman centurion, and said that the Holy Spirit had made no distinction between Jew and Gentile. Barnabas and Paul reported the signs and wonders God had done through them among the gentiles—those not circumcised.

James announced the decision of the conference, a compromise decision: Gentiles could be baptized into the church without first being circumcised, but once in the church these gentiles had to observe the Jewish dietary and other sanctity laws. This decision was to be reported to all the churches.

Apparently the earlier provocative actions of Stephen had so alienated other parties in the Jesus movement that the

Hellenists were not welcome in the others' assemblies; as we have seen, they were not represented at this one. This same omission is apparent in a creed later incorporated into Paul's correspondence with the Corinthians. The creed, in 1 Corinthians 15, likely indicates that the conference and the creed's writing took place at almost the same time early in the church's life.

Paul states the creed as having been agreed to by all parties who were represented in Jerusalem:

> *For I delivered to you as of first importance what I also received,*
> *that Christ died for our sins in accordance with the scriptures,*
> *that he was buried,*
> *that he was raised on the third day in accordance with the scriptures,*
> *and that he appeared to Cephas [Peter],*
> *then to the twelve,*
> *then he appeared to five hundred brethren at one time most of whom are still alive though some have fallen asleep,*
> *then he appeared to James,*
> *then to all the apostles,*
> *last of all, as to one untimely born, he appeared also to me (1 Cor 15:3–8)*

It seems clear that this creed is not a mere recounting of recorded appearances of Jesus to his followers. From other sources we know that Jesus appeared to Peter (Cephas) and to the Twelve (reduced to Eleven by the death of Judas). The appearance to the five hundred brethren may have referred to the coming of the Holy Spirit to the Brethren in Jerusalem at Pentecost. Additional appearances not included in this creed are also recorded in the gospels—to the women, to Mary Magdalene, and to the men of Emmaus, among others. There is also the appearance of "The Son of Humankind" to Stephen at the moment of his death. But there are no recorded appearances in other parts of the New Testament "to James" or to "all the apostles." Clearly this creedal statement is not meant to be a record of all of Jesus' appearances. It has some other purpose.

The words with which this creed begins—*"I delivered to you as of first importance what I also received"*—help to explain its intent. This was a common Jewish formula for stating agreements worked out following disputes within their communities. The same formula was used when Paul talked about the Lord's Supper (1 Cor 11:23). This creed therefore refers to the authentic leadership within the Christian movement, identifying it with the persons named and with the groups they led. This decision is then to be transmitted to all the churches. The best way to catalogue this apparent jumble of names and groups is to see it as a series of three phrases:

a) Cephas and the Twelve

b) Five hundred Brethren and James

c) All the Apostles and Paul

From other New Testament sources, we find that arranging the statement in this manner comes very close to the historic order in which Jesus' appearances took place. He first appeared to Peter, then to the twelve, together and singly. The appearance to "five hundred brethren" precedes the otherwise unknown appearance to James. The "Apostles," as we shall see, had come together as a group before Jesus appeared to Paul and designated him as their leader.

This arrangement of the creed puts focus on the primary leadership of the early Christian movement—three leaders were enumerated as the authentic leaders within the church, James, Peter, and Paul. These three groups to whom the resurrected Jesus had come were authorized to carry out ministry in his name, the Twelve, the Brethren, and the Apostles. This creed, then, was the result of the early Christian movement, at some indeterminate time, agreeing that these were the only certified persons and parties entrusted with Jesus' continuing work.

We know that the three leaders were integral to the spread of the Jesus movement. But a question must be faced: Did such groups or parties as Brethren and Apostles really exist? Searching the New Testament produces more than shadows and echoes of their presence.

In the earliest days of the Jesus movement, the role of persons and parties in leadership was largely undifferentiated. But in the altercation between the "Hebrews" and the "Hellenists," the "one" church divided into two groups, and also retained a third party, the original leadership of the Twelve of Galilee. When the Apostles later appeared as a distinct party in the church with a distinct mission, four parties in total were then at work in Jesus' ministry.

The clearest way of seeing this is to look at the books contained in the New Testament. The Letters of John are different in style and substance from the letters of Paul. The Letter of James is different from the other two sets of letters. Above all, we have four gospels, each related to one another but each having its own theological and ethical emphases.

We have other indications of the presence of these parties. In describing the work of the church in Corinth, Paul wrote that some Corinthians said *"I belong to Paul"*; others said, *"I belong to Apollos"*; others, *"'I belong to Cephas,' or 'I belong to Christ'"* (1 Cor 1:12). Four parties are mentioned here—Apostles, Disciples, Brethren (if we credit that the "Christ party" is the party of Torah-observant Jews), and a fourth, not denoted above, the party of Apollos (who was a Hellenist from Alexandria and who took over the leadership of the Hellenist party from the others).

Further evidence comes in 1 Cor 9:5. Paul was answering charges against him lodged by the Corinthian church, and he cried in exasperation, *"Do we not have the right to be accompanied by a wife, as do the other apostles and the brothers of the Lord and Cephas?"* Again, three groups of missioners—"apostles," "brothers of the Lord," and "Cephas."

This mass of evidence of the presence of contending parties in the early church constitutes a revolutionary change in thinking about the nature of Christian mission in its first forty years. Most interpretations of these years presuppose a time of rapid success for the church built upon individual achievements and heroic faith, an era when the church was inexorably led by the spirit of Christ, an epoch when for the last time in its history the church was single-minded about its aims and goals.

The discovery of four distinct parties within the early Jesus movement requires a rethinking of these assumptions. Studying each of the four major groups produces questions about their beginning, their organization, their mission, their belief systems, their ethical systems, their distinguishing features, their surviving literature, and their termination.

Altogether such a perspective results in a new understanding about the growth and spread of the Christian movement in its first four decades. It only in part came through individual achievement and heroic faith, important as these were. It also came when parties with different perspectives organized themselves to spread the faith. They had different organs of governance, they set different goals and targets for their actions, they had distinctive doctrines, and they had beginnings and, for two of them, endings. In the coming pages each party will be described in detail. We will use accepted markers to differentiate among them. We will see that each becomes a specific part of a greater movement. The final result is a new paradigm of the complex epoch in the early Christian movement when the faith first emerged.

Table 1 gives a broad outline of what is to come in describing each of the four identifiable movements in the emerging church. The columns represent each of the four parties, and rows represent the thirteen major categories of differences found among the parties. Each party had a beginning event, and, for two of the parties, terminating events. The other eleven categories represent major issues which highlight how the parties differed in their approaches and writings.

Table 1. Characteristics of the Four Parties in the Early Jesus Movement.

Parties	The Twelve Disciples	Brethren	Hellenists	Apostles
Beginning Event				
Governance				
Mission Targets				
Composition of Party				
Places of Worship				
Circumcision				
Food Laws				
Marriage Laws				
Theological Self-Understanding				
Role of Jesus				
Primary Ethical Principle				
Writings				
Terminating Event				

The substance of differences will be explained in the coming chapters and the table will be filled in column by column as we progress, culminating when the entire table will be completed substantively in Chapters 5 and 6.

This approach to understanding the earliest four some-times-quite-divisive parties within the Jesus movement recognizes that the overall movement was both unified and divided as it sought to resolve the doctrinal and organizational problems faced by the early churches. It also clarifies where and how social circumstances and events affected the Jesus movement. Key writings generated by each of the parties underscore the competitive theologies, ethics, and collective and household practices found in the churches.

The perspectives underlying this work provide additional understanding about where contemporary Christian ideas and practices originated, evolved, and continue to affect contemporary church organization, theology, ethics, and practices. These perspectives also challenge contemporary Christians to re-think how their church organization can be more productive in affecting Christians' commitments to living in ways more compatible with increasing the love and caring exemplified by Jesus in their intimate assemblies, their communities, and their worlds.

CHAPTER 2

The Disciples:
Peter and the Twelve

Simon–Cephas–Peter

Simon of Bethsaida first met Jesus of Nazareth when both
were in Judea in the company of John the Baptist. Along with
his brother Andrew, Simon had gone to Judea in response to
the preaching of the Baptist. These few verses tell us a great
deal about Simon (Jn 1:35-42).

> The next day again John was standing with two of his
> disciples; and he looked at Jesus as he walked, and said,
> "Behold, the Lamb of God!" The two disciples heard him
> say this, and they followed Jesus. Jesus turned, and saw
> them following, and said to them, "What do you seek?"
> And they said to him, "Rabbi" (which means Teacher),
> "where are you staying?" He said to them, "Come and
> see." They came and saw where he was staying; and they
> stayed with him that day, for it was about the tenth hour.

> One of the two who heard John speak, and followed
> him, was Andrew, Simon Peter's brother. He first found
> his brother Simon, and said to him, "We have found the
> Messiah" (which means Christ). He brought him to Jesus.
> Jesus looked at him, and said, "So you are Simon the son of
> John? You shall be called Cephas" (which means Peter).

Simon was from Bethsaida, a fishing village located on the northern shore of the Sea of Galilee, east of Capernaum. It was one of thirteen fishing harbors on the sea. Interestingly enough, Bethsaida is mentioned more often in the New Testament than any city except Jerusalem and Capernaum.

Simon's name itself is curious. In this form it is more Greek than Hebrew. Simon's Hebrew name would have been Shimon, transliterated into Symeon, but he was rarely called that. Andrew, his brother, and Philip, his fellow townsman, are never given Hebrew names. Sometime in his life Simon had been given a nickname: he was called "The Rock." Whether Jesus gave him this nickname or simply acknowledged that he already had it is not clear from this passage in John nor from Matthew 16:18, where Jesus says, "I tell you, you are Peter, and on this rock I will build my church." Two translations are given for Simon's nickname. Among Jewish speaking people he is called Cephas, among Greek speaking peoples he is called Peter. The implication has to be that these Galilean families were subject to strong Greek influence.

Indications are also strong that Simon's family was reasonably well-to-do. According to the picture given in Mark and Luke, their fishing operation was fairly large-scale. They worked in partnership with James and John, the sons of Zebedee (Lk 5:7, 10), and they employed others (Mk 1:20).

Fishing was an important industry in the world of their time. Fish was a dietary source used in place of meat. The wealthy were able to eat fresh fish. Salted fish were the delicacies in the diet of the poor.

Bethsaida and Capernaum were both well-situated to provide salted fish. These small Galilean cities were near the "salt fish factory" located in Magdala, a village on the sea a few miles west of Capernaum. As far as we know, this was the only such factory on the northern coast of the Sea of Galilee. Here fish were dried and salted, then shipped to market.

Some time before Jesus came to Capernaum for the first time, Simon and Andrew had moved their fishing operation to Capernaum from Bethsaida. The reason for the move would be understood by any business person–they made the move in order to reduce their tax obligations. Bethsaida belonged to the territory of Herod Philip, while Capernaum and Magdala were in the territory of Herod Antipas. To bring fish from Philip's territory to Antipas', from Bethsaida to Magdala, the fishermen had to cross the territorial line. The taxing house in Capernaum taxed them heavily for this privilege. The smart thing to do was to move from Bethsaida to Capernaum and set up business there. Simon and Andrew did this smart thing.

They moved into the house owned by Simon's wife's mother. This was a sumptuous house, as any one who visits Capernaum today can discover. Known since the fourth century as the House of Peter, it is larger than most of the other houses excavated in Capernaum. This house became their headquarters. It also became the Galilean headquarters of Jesus after he moved from Judea to Galilee following the arrest of John the Baptist.

Putting these factors together offers a good look at the family of Simon and Andrew. Jerome Murphy-O'Conner (the major source for much of this material) summarizes it:

> Simon and Andrew came from a prosperous, assimilated Jewish middle-class family. Speaking both Aramaic and Greek, they were brought up to serve in an administrative as well as a practical role in an essential major industry. They knew how to plan and organize. As experienced businessmen, they were astute enough to move their home in order to take advantage of a tax break. Such shrewdness, one can be sure, also manifested itself in the way they handled competition from the many other fishermen on the Sea of Galilee and the Jordan River. They were anything but "uneducated, common men" (Murphy-O'Conner).

When Jesus came to Galilee following the arrest of John the Baptizer, one of the first things he did was to call Simon,

Andrew, James, and John to be his followers. *"Follow me,"* he said, *"and I will make you fishers of men"* (Mk 1:17). This was an unusual act on Jesus' part. Disciples usually sought out masters to whom to attach themselves and not the other way around. But Jesus invited these men to be his disciples, and they responded to his call.

They followed him around the synagogues of Galilee, and saw him heal the sick and cast out demons. They watched as he invited others to join his group. They heard and remembered his teaching. They embarked with him onto a boat, and were awed when he stilled the storm that threatened to capsize them. They participated when he fed five thousand people with just a few loaves and fishes. A few of them climbed the Mount of Transfiguration with him. All of them followed him when he turned his face to Jerusalem for one final solemn celebration of Passover.

Simon was often the spokesperson for the group, although his quick tongue got him into frequent trouble. One such moment occurred on the road to Caesarea Philippi. *"Who do you say that I am?"* Jesus had asked. Peter replied, *"You are the Christ."* It was true, but Jesus did not yet want to be known by that title. He told Simon in effect to keep his mouth shut about it (Mk 8:27–30). Simon spoke too quickly at the moment of transfiguration. Seeing Jesus with Moses and Elijah, all the practical Simon could think of was "Let us build you three tents" (Mk 9:5). He certainly spoke too quickly following Jesus' arrest in Jerusalem. When challenged in the temple for speaking with a Galilean accent, he retorted, *"I do not know the man."* He was sorry ever after for that (Mk 14:66–72). Yet it was around this able, articulate, talented businessman that the Jesus movement first coalesced. Simon became known by the title Jesus had bestowed upon him, "The Rock."

The formation of the group called "The Twelve," otherwise known as "The Disciples," began in the Galilean ministry of Jesus, and it was capped with the appearance of the risen Christ *"first to Cephas and then to the Twelve"* (1 Cor

15:3). This Galilean group was one of the two earliest groups within the Christian movement (the other was composed of his Judean followers), so, as we describe them, we are describing the Jesus movement as it was in its beginning.

The movement had its headquarters in Jerusalem; just as Simon had moved the headquarters of his fishing enterprise from Bethsaida to Capernaum, he also moved the headquarters of the Jesus enterprise from Capernaum to Jerusalem. Many people were part of this group. The eleven disciples who followed Jesus to Jerusalem were certainly part of it (Acts 1:13–14). They were joined by the women who had come up with them from Galilee and by other men who accompanied them (Joseph Barsabbas and Matthias are mentioned by name.)

Others who lived in Judea are also named as being part of this group in Jerusalem. Mary, the mother of Jesus, and Jesus's brothers specifically are named. Mary, whose care had been assigned to the Beloved Disciple, had been living in Jerusalem, as were unnamed brothers of Jesus. In this group, therefore, some had been with Jesus in Galilee while others were residents of Jerusalem and environs.

The first act the Disciples performed after returning from the Mount of Olives where Jesus had left them for the last time (Acts 1:10–12) was to restore their number to its original twelve. The number had been reduced to eleven by the treachery of Judas and his subsequent suicide.

Specific qualifications for filling the position were set up. The candidate must be a man: none of the women in the group were to be considered for this office. He had to be a man who had accompanied the eleven during the time of Jesus' Galilean ministry, who had been with him, as they said, *"from the baptism of John until the day Jesus was taken from us"* (Acts 1:21). His selection would qualify him to be a witness with the others to Jesus' resurrection. Acting upon a well-used precedent in Jewish communities, they filled the position by lot. Putting forth two candidates who fulfilled their requirements, Joseph Barsabbas Justus and Matthias, they let the Lord make the selection. The lot fell upon Matthias, and he was enrolled with the other eleven.

Their original ministry was one of teaching and healing like that of Jesus. Peter and John were reported to have gone to the temple and healed a man lame from birth (Acts 3:1-10). They were arrested for this act and brought to trial before the council by the high priest of the family of Annas. In the trial they proclaimed that the man had been healed "*by the name of Jesus Christ of Nazareth.*" They further declared that "*there was no other name under heaven by which salvation could come*" (Acts 4:10–12). Having no charge to lay against Peter and John, the council freed them, sent them on their way, and admonished them not to preach and heal further. The two Disciples refused to obey, saying that "*we cannot but speak of what we have seen and heard*" (4:20).

This scene is designed to be typical of the work of the Disciples. It points up the following about them:

1. They were constituted as a fellowship of prayer: "*all these devoted themselves to prayer*" (Acts 1:14). It was repeated, "*they were going up to the temple at the hour of prayer*"(Acts 3:1 and reaffirmed in 4:23–31), when, after their report of their success in court, the fellowship prayed to God with such power that the place in which they gathered was shaken, and they were filled with the Holy Spirit.

2. They continued the work of teaching, preaching and healing which they had been commissioned to do by the risen Jesus. They emphasized the miraculous work being done in the name of the Jesus, for not only was the man healed but they praised God that God "*had stretched out thy hand to heal and signs and wonders are performed through the name of thy holy servant Jesus*" (Acts 4:30).

3. They centered their work around the temple in Jerusalem, to which they went regularly to preach, to pray, and to sacrifice.

4. Their other practices were performed in the manner of Torah-observant Jews. They adhered to the food laws of Judaism and circumcised their male infants; the recording of the circumcision of the infant Jesus is indicative of that (Lk 2:21: "*at the end of eight days he was circumcised*"). They celebrated Pentecost, which was originally a Jewish holy day, the fiftieth day after Passover. Their celebration of the Passover took on overtones of the Lord's Supper. They believed that Jesus ate and drank with them in this manner after his resurrection (Acts 10:41).

5. Governance of the group reflected Jewish patterns. Their acknowledged leader was Cephas, otherwise known as Simon Peter. Around him was the larger council of the Twelve. Beyond them was a larger assembly of seventy, or seventy-two men who acted in the name of the Twelve (Lk 10:1).

6. They found a platform for presenting their message when they went into the synagogues of the Jews to proclaim that the Jesus who had been crucified was indeed the Christ for whom Judaism had waited so long and whom God had now sent into their midst.

   It was not unusual that they would seek out a synagogue to present their message. The Judaism of 30 C.E. was sufficiently tolerant, or, to put it another way, sufficiently crisscrossed with conflicting viewpoints about the truth of faith, to permit any to speak to the many within the precincts of their synagogues.

   Preaching in the synagogue was supplemented by teaching in the temple. But to preach in the temple quickly developed into a more perilous method for presenting their message. Soon they were brought before priests and courts to defend the point of view they espoused. As they remembered Jesus' own trial before the priests and then Pilate, they were emboldened to use their trials as bully pulpits from which to present their message about Jesus. These accounts of their trials circulated through Jerusalem and became a focal point of the Disciples' witness.

7. They considered themselves to be the successors of all Israel, as their name, The Twelve, implied. Peter affirmed this by identifying the Disciples with "the God of Abraham and of Isaac and of Jacob, the God of our fathers." Since 721 B.C.E., there had not been twelve tribes in Israel. In that year, Assyrian armies destroyed Samaria, the capital of the Northern Kingdom of Israel. This kingdom had consisted of ten of the twelve original tribes of Israel, and the Assyrians had dragged the survivors of the battles into exile. But through Jesus, the twelve tribes were reconstituted in the persons of the twelve Disciples, and together they considered themselves "the true Israel." The number "twelve" was so important to them that, when one of the original Twelve (Judas) was lost, they moved quickly to restore their group to that number by enrolling Matthias with the original eleven.

8. They used the special name "servant" for Jesus. This was in fulfilment of the "servant passages" in the prophecy of Isaiah, especially 42:7 and 53 (Jeremiah 31:17,20 and Hosea 11:1–8 prefigured the Suffering Servant before Isaiah articulated it). The earlier passage talked of a mission to the ends of the earth. The latter said that the mission was to be carried out by a servant who was *"despised and rejected, by whose stripes we are healed."* The "servant passages" of Isaiah played a strong part in Jesus' announcements of his coming death in Jerusalem (*"If any man would come after me, let him deny himself and take up his cross and follow me"* [Mk 8:34]; *"how is it written of the Son of man, that he should suffer many things and be treated with contempt?"* [Mk 9:9]; *"The Son of man will be delivered into the hands of men, and they will kill him; and when he is killed, after three days he will rise"* [Mk 9:31]; *"Behold, we are going up to Jerusalem;*

and the Son of man will be delivered to the chief priests and the scribes, and they will condemn him to death, and deliver him to the Gentiles; and they will mock him, and spit upon him, and scourge him, and kill him; and after three days he will rise" [Mk 10:33–34]). It also helped to fashion Mark's account of Jesus' crucifixion, which underlies all the gospel narratives of Jesus' passion.

9. If the Disciples were to fulfil Jesus' ministry, they would have to do the same: be willing to suffer as their lord had done. *"If you will be my disciples,"* Jesus had said, *"you must take up your cross and follow me"* (Mk 8:34). The "servant" Christology provided the Disciples not only with their message but also with the methodology to carry it out. Some of the Twelve took it literally. James the Son of Zebedee, was killed by Herod Agrippa, and there is a strong historical memory that Peter met this same fate in Rome. But this emphasis seems to have dropped out of New Testament thinking before the time of the destruction of the temple in 70 c.e.—perhaps it was too stringent a message to attract many converts and it probably led to the early demise of the Peter movement. It played only a secondary role in the theologies of the other groups that gathered in Jesus' name.

10. They emphasized the necessity of repentance on the part of Jewish people. Since the people had had a hand in Jesus' crucifixion, only by repenting of this sin could they become part of Jesus' new fellowship. The language the Twelve used against the people of the synagogues was strong: *"You delivered (him) up and denied (him) in the presence of Pilate, when he had decided to release him"* (Acts 3:13); *"you killed the Author of life"* (3:14); *"you acted in ignorance, as did your rulers"* (3:17). When gentiles began to respond to their message, they extended their proclamation by announcing that everyone who believed

in Jesus received forgiveness of sins through his name (10:43).

11. The resurrection of Jesus had a special meaning for the Twelve. In raising Jesus from the dead, they said, God was giving the Jews one more chance to repent, return, and become part of the new Israel that rose with Jesus from the grave and of which they were the representatives. Forgiveness for them did not carry the same meaning it was to have later for Paul. Paul thought that the resurrection of Jesus offered forgiveness for all sins. The Twelve seemed to restrict "forgiveness." The chief sin, according to the Twelve, was that the leadership of the Jewish nation had crucified Jesus. Forgiveness was the means by which those Jews who recognized what they had done to Jesus were welcomed anew by God into Jesus' new fellowship, reconstituted Israel. When gentiles recognized that the Lord of Life had been crucified, they too were granted repentance unto life (Acts 11:18).

12. They considered the risen Jesus to be judge of all the living and the dead (10:42). To quote from the Confession of 1967 of the Presbyterian Church: "Christ's life and teachings judged the goodness, religious aspirations, and national hopes" of all persons and societies.... "His judgment discloses the ultimate seriousness of life and gives promise to God's final victory over the power of sin and death" (C67, 9.09, 9.11).

The Disciples moved quickly beyond Jerusalem in their work. They found converts to their message in the synagogues of Joppa, Caesarea, Damascus, and Antioch, and they carried their mission to the island of Cyprus.

ii

The first change in the orientation of the group occurred soon after they began to spread their message abroad. In a virulently contentious moment in the history of the Jesus movement, "Hellenists" and "Hebrews" had separated from each other.

There were two kinds of synagogues in Jerusalem. There were the traditional Torah-observant synagogues. Their constituents spoke Aramaic in their homes and business and used Hebrew as their language of worship. There were also Hellenist synagogues which served the Greek-speaking Jewish people who lived in Jerusalem. These synagogues conducted their services in Greek for Jews who used that language as their primary language at home and in their business life; they read from the Septuagint, the official Greek translation of their scriptures, and they offered their prayers in Greek.

There is a question as to how many Hellenist synagogues were in Jerusalem. Acts 6:9 can be read as referring to only one synagogue, that of the Freedmen, which included persons from Alexandria, Cyrene, Cilicia, and Asia. Or it could refer to as many as four synagogues: that of the Freedmen and synagogues for, respectively, the Cyrenians, the Alexandrians, and those from Cilicia and Asia. Given the size and ethnic backgrounds of the Greek-speaking Jewish community in Jerusalem, it is more likely that each ethnic group had established its own synagogue for their own use and for the use of their fellow countrymen when they visited in the Holy City. Simon of Cyrene, who carried Jesus' cross to Golgotha, was a farmer who lived in Jerusalem and who most likely was connected with the synagogue of the Cyrenians.

The Jesus movement had already made inroads into each type of synagogue. But long-standing cultural strains between the two types of people, Torah-observant Jews and their Hellenist co-religionists, had arisen between the two groups in the Jesus movement. The fight broke out over a small issue—the Hellenists claimed that their widows were being short-changed by the Jewish leaders in the daily distribution of food. The dispute escalated when in a speech

(Acts 6–8) Stephen declared that the Hebrew practice of the faith was deficient in major ways, and Jews rose up to stone Stephen. With Stephen's death, the two factions split irrevocably. Peter and the others from Galilee continued to see themselves as part of the Hebrew bloc.

iii

This was soon to change. A dramatic confrontation between Peter and the gentile Cornelius made the Twelve rethink some of their practices. The story is told at great length—over two chapters, 10 and 11—in the Book of Acts.

Peter, traveling along the coast of the Mediterranean through Joppa and Lydda and visiting the congregations there, was unexpectedly invited by a Roman centurion named Cornelius to come to his house to stay for a while. Acts describes Cornelius in this way: *"He was a devout man who feared God with all his household, gave alms liberally to the people, and prayed constantly to God"* (Acts 10:2). This is the classic description of the group of people known in the synagogues as "godfearers," men and their families who were attracted to the Jewish faith but who themselves had never been circumcised as proselytes. According to Cornelius' own story, he sent the invitation to Peter because he had been instructed to do so in a vision given him by God (10:1–8).

In the meantime Peter himself had had a perplexing vision. He had seen the heavens opened and something like a great sheet let down by four corners upon the earth. In it were all kinds of animals, reptiles, and birds of the air. A voice told Peter to *"Kill and eat."* Peter protested, *"I have never eaten anything that is common or unclean."* The voice replied, *"What God has cleansed, you must not call common"* (10:9–16).

In the next moment Peter knew the meaning of his vision. The men from Cornelius knocked on his door with the invitation to visit in the centurion's house, and Peter accompanied them to Caesarea. Cornelius told of his vision, and Peter told of his. As they spoke together, to the amazement of the whole company the Holy Spirit came upon the gentiles. Peter was so convinced that God had planned and carried out the event that he cried, *"Can anyone forbid these people water for baptizing?"* Receiving no negative answer from the awed assemblage, Peter baptized Cornelius, his household, and his friends into the faith (Acts 10:17–48; the story is largely repeated in 11:1–18).

Five centuries and more of the universal Jewish practices of circumcision and of food laws were discarded in that one moment. To that moment, Peter and the rest of the Disciples had had fellowship only with followers of Jesus from the Hebrew-speaking synagogues. Now a godfearer, a gentile who was not first a proselyte, was accorded the privileges of their fellowship. For the first time a gentile was baptized into the Jesus movement without first being circumcised, and for the first time a disciple ate a meal with a gentile without first following the food laws prescribed by his forebears. The revolution that erupted in these events is breathtaking. When Peter visited Cornelius in Caesarea, the face of the Christian faith was changed forever.

From this time on, the Twelve and the Brothers of Jesus became alienated from each other. Peter had broken the most important tenets of Jewish faith. The Torah-observant Hebrews who had become part of the Jesus movement were aghast at this, and they continued to hold fast to what they believed was the true interpretation of Jesus' intent. When Peter and his followers in Antioch ate with gentile followers of Jesus, the party of James sent a delegation to this congregation to request that Peter and the rest cease what they were doing (Gal 2:11–13). Fearing "the circumcision party," Peter did as they asked.

iv

This party of the Twelve came to an early and strange end. Herod Agrippa, the grandson of Herod who was appointed ruler of Judea when Pontius Pilate was deposed in 36 C.E., soon began to persecute the growing Jesus movement. *"The king laid violent hands upon some who belonged to the church, and he killed James the brother of John with the sword. Seeing that it pleased the Jews, he proceeded to arrest Peter also"* (Acts 12:1–3).

The story that follows this (Acts 12:3–17) is one of the strangest in the New Testament. It says that Peter was arrested and placed in prison. Without announcement, Peter was released from his bonds and escorted out of the prison by an angel. Peter made his way to the door of a house where his followers were staying. Seeing him appear so unexpectedly, they at first refused to let him enter the house, but then they welcomed him. Peter described how the Lord had brought him out of the prison. Then he said, *"Tell this to James and the brethren."* Then, said Acts, *"he departed and went to another place."*

Where he went we do not know. Some have supposed that this is the story of Peter's death, but that is not possible because Peter turns up in other places in the New Testament. It was not Peter's death that is described here, but it is the story of a death—the death of Peter's party, the Twelve. After this persecution by Agrippa, the Twelve as a group appear no more in New Testament stories. Some individuals had lived through the persecution, but the energy that had fueled the group was exhausted. No longer were they active in Jerusalem and its environs. They founded no new congregations anywhere. When James the brother of John, one of the original Twelve, died, the group made no attempt to fill his place among the Twelve as they had done earlier at the death of Judas (Acts 1:15–26). Leadership in the Christian mission passed fully into the hands of "James and the brethren."

V

On the basis of the above, we can begin to fill in the thirteen cells in the second column of Table 2. The beginning event

Table 2. Summary: The Party of the Twelve on Thirteen Major Issues.

Parties	The Twelve Disciples	Brethren	Hellenists	Apostles
Beginning Event	Jesus' call in Galilee			
Governance	Cephas; The Twelve, The Assembly of 70			
Mission Targets	Synagogues in Galilee, Gaza			
Composition of Party	Jewish men in leadership, some women			
Places of Worship	Temple, synagogues, house churches			
Circumcision	Jewish men and proselytes before the Jerusalem Conference, only Jewish men after			
Food Laws	Kept, then did not			
Marriage Laws	Married Jewish women			
Theological Self-Understanding	Successor to Israel			
Role of Jesus	Servant of God			
Primary Ethical Principle	"Take up cross, follow me"			

Parties	The Twelve Disciples	Brethren	Hellenists	Apostles
Writings	Mark 1st Peter			
Terminating Event	Death of leaders under Herod Agrippa			

was clearly Jesus' call in Galilee. Its governance put Peter as the leader, assisted by eleven others. Its mission was to synagogues in the smaller places in Palestine, with less emphasis on those in Jerusalem. Each of the twelve was a man, and their followers were mostly men, with a few women. As far as we know, women did not become a part of the twelve, but they were in the congregations of the Disciples. Except for a brief encounter with Cornelius the centurion, the three major Torah-based laws regarding food, circumcision, and marriage were probably kept. The places of worship were in the Hebrew tradition—synagogues and the Temple—but also some congregations held fellowship meetings in their houses.

The Twelve saw Jesus as the suffering servant of God. As such they gave Old Testament religion a new orientation by remembering Jesus' words, "*take up your cross and follow me.*" This position had a long history in biblical Judaism. Isaiah of Babylon had articulated it in the 6th century B.C.E. in chapters 42 and 53 of his prophecy. Isaiah's message had been built upon earlier prophecies by Hosea (11:1–8) and Jeremiah (32:17–20.) It had been given more recent expression in the scrolls found at Qumran (Knohl, 2008). In understanding Jesus' role in the social life of the Hebrews' religion, this theological stance is fundamental. It provided Old Testament authority to the beliefs of the Disciples. It fed their belief that Jesus was sent from God to be God's suffering servant. Jesus' call to his followers to suffer and to sacrifice themselves for his mission deserved to be emulated. This is the essential ethic of the Peter party. Such ethical and theological principles saw their primary written expression in the Gospel of Mark.

The party in its evangelizing ministry seemed to fall apart after some of its leaders were executed and Peter was imprisoned by Herod Agrippa. But Peter escaped the imprisonment and was a figure in several of Paul's letters. Other than in these letters, what happened to Peter after his imprisonment does not appear in any detail in the written records of the New Testament. Paul talks about visiting with Disciples in various places, mostly where they had been successful in Peter's original ministry outside Jerusalem. In other words, the ministry of the Twelve continued in places where Peter had established congregations, and a few beyond this area. But they do not figure overall except in this relatively limited area.

vi

Still, the footprints of Peter do not quite disappear from the New Testament.

One set lead Peter to Antioch. This story is told in Paul's Letter to the Galatians, and its telling brings together three of the parties in the Jesus movement. The passage quoted is only a fragment of the total event. Paul wrote:

> *When Cephas came to Antioch I opposed him to his face, because he stood condemned. For before certain men came from James, he ate with the Gentiles; but when they came he drew back and separated himself, fearing the circumcision party. And with him the rest of the Jews acted insincerely, so that even Barnabas was carried away by their insincerity. But when I saw that they were not straightforward about the truth of the gospel, I said to Cephas before them all, "If you, though a Jew, live like a Gentile and not like a Jew, how can you compel the*

Gentiles to live like Jews?" We ourselves, who are Jews by birth and not Gentile sinners, know that a man is not justified by works of the law but through faith in Jesus Christ (Gal 2:11–16).

Here Paul breaks off his story. What we have tells of a wide-ranging struggle between Paul and Peter that took place in Antioch.

Years before in Jerusalem Paul had previously met both Peter and James. He had returned to that city after he believed that he had received a call from God to preach Christ to the gentiles (Gal 1:15–16). Previous to receiving that call Paul had by his own admission *"persecuted the church of God violently"* (Gal 1:13) and he was examined by Peter and James to determine his trustworthiness in preaching the gospel. It was not immediately granted. Paul was placed on a three-year probationary period, which he spent in Arabia and Damascus.

He returned to Jerusalem a second time and met with the two pillars of the church. This time he received the credential that he had sought. *"He who once persecuted us is now preaching the faith he once tried to destroy"* (Gal 1:23). Shortly after, Paul went to the Galatian cities of Derbe, Lystra, and Iconium, and ministered successfully in this area. Peter went to Caesarea where he met with Cornelius, the retired centurion. Both Peter and Paul, independently, had concluded that God through Jesus had broken the long taboo against Jews and gentiles eating together. When Peter arrived in Antioch after he had escaped from Herod's jail, he and Barnabas joined the gentiles in the Jesus movement in Antioch in partaking of the symbolic supper of bread and wine.

Then, we are told, *"certain men came from James"* (Gal 2:12a). What they said caused both Peter and Barnabas to *"draw back and separate themselves, fearing the circumcision party"* (Gal 2:12b). When they followed Peter's example by drawing back, Paul said, the rest of the Jews acted insincerely, so that even Barnabas was carried away by their insincerity. Paul was incensed, and he reprimanded Peter to his face.

Why Peter withdrew from this common fellowship is not addressed in Paul's account. Maybe he was succumbing to the pressure of a colleague, James, who by Peter's own account had succeeded him in the primary leadership of the movement. Peter is reported to have said when he emerged from prison, *"Tell this to James and to the brethren"* (Acts 12:17).

On the other hand, maybe Peter was caught in a dilemma that he could not resolve. Perhaps the men from James had told Peter that his act was causing harm to members of James' Hebrew party who lived in Jerusalem. Luke talked about men *"hating you and excluding you, and reviling you, and casting out your name as evil on account of the Son of Humankind"* (6:22). This is a description of the process set up in synagogues for dealing with schismatic members. First, they were hated by their fellow Jews and had to withstand all the hatred that religious people can pile upon other religious people. Then, they were excluded, so that they could have no more dealings with their former comrades. They could not sell or buy goods from them, they could not marry their daughters to the sons of their former friends and fellow religionists, could not attend their funerals, and on their deaths could not be buried in cemeteries "with their fathers." When their names were "cast out as evil," this was the last step in the exclusionary process. Their names were erased from the synagogue rolls, and they were treated by other Jews as if they were dead. "Do not eat with gentiles," James was saying to Peter. "If you do and the word of it comes back to Jerusalem, you are doing irreparable harm to those you love." No wonder Peter pulled back.

We also see Peter when he appeared in the Jerusalem Conference of Acts 15. He told the assembled Apostles and elders that by his mouth God gave the Holy Spirit to gentiles. Since this is true, Peter asked, why do you want to put the yoke (of the law) upon the neck of the Disciples? James quoted Peter's speech as he made his momentous decision that gentiles need not be circumcised. As he did so, he called Peter by his Hebrew name, Symeon (Acts 15:6-14).

Under the name Cephas, Peter appeared in Paul's correspondence with his Corinthian church. Apparently the Twelve had succeeded in establishing a congregation in Corinth. Noting the divisions that had arisen within the Jesus movement in Corinth, Paul said that some of them claimed, *"I belong to Paul,...I belong to Cephas"* (1 Cor 1:12). Paul also notes that, when Cephas was in Corinth, he was accompanied by his wife (1 Cor 9:5).

Peter was not mentioned as being in Rome when Paul saluted his friends in the Roman congregations (Romans 16:1-16). Had Peter been there at the time Paul wrote his letter, presumably about 57 c.e., he would surely have sent a greeting to Peter.

Yet, in a strange way, Peter was in Rome at that time. The Gospel of Mark was composed about the time that Paul's letter was received in Rome. This gospel set Peter, in all his flawed grandeur, into the heart of the Jesus movement.

> Peter was the first one in Galilee called to follow Jesus: Peter the called.
>
> He offered Jesus a place to stay in his own home: Peter the host.
>
> He saw Jesus teach and heal and cause the dead to rise: Peter the witness.
>
> He sat among those whom Jesus fed in the wilderness and at the table of the Last Supper: Peter the privileged.
>
> He was the first to call Jesus "the Christ": Peter the insightful.
>
> When Jesus was transfigured before them, Peter was the one who wanted to erect three tents for the visitors to stay in: Peter the practical.

When Jesus said that all his disciples would desert him in his hour of greatest need, Peter had protested that he would remain faithful: Peter the impetuous.

He joined Jesus in his prayer in Gethsemane: Peter the man of prayer.

He was the first to fall asleep that night: Peter the tired.

When Peter was outside the courtroom of Jerusalem, he denied that he knew the man on trial; three times he denied it: Peter the denier.

After he denied his Lord, he broke down and wept: Peter the forgiven.

The Gospel of Mark, written in Rome three decades after Jesus' resurrection, fused Jesus and Peter together for all time. We cannot think of one without thinking of the other.

CHAPTER 3

The Brothers of the Lord

That the leadership of the Christian movement in Jerusalem had passed from Peter to James is seen in two passages in Paul's Letter to the Galatians. When Paul first went up to Jerusalem to have his credentials for mission checked by the church leaders there, he tells us that he consulted first with Peter and then with James (Gal 1:18–19). On his second visit, *"after fourteen years,"* the order is reversed: *"James and Cephas and John gave to me...the right hand of fellowship"* (Gal 2:9). Such a reversal of position between Peter and James indicates that there had been a shift in power in the early church. This is demonstrated even more clearly in the Council of Jerusalem, dated around 47 C.E., about three years after Agrippa's persecution. In that Council, James is the presiding officer and pre-eminent voice, and Peter and the others play subordinate though important roles.

James' group sat for its picture in the Pentecost story of the Book of Acts. Judea was squarely in the middle of the portrait. Jerusalem was considered the focus of the faith, the central point from which faith emanated and to which the faithful were to return for strength and nourishment.

Surrounding this core on the east and north were the Hebrew-speaking synagogues of Persia, Media, Elam, and Mesopotamia. To the north and west were those of Cappadocia, Pontus, and Asia, to the south Egypt and Cyrene. Arabians, Libyans, and "visitors from Rome, both Jews and proselytes" are also listed. These last may have taken the faith with them when they returned home and preached it to their fellow Jews. Large concentric circles, with Jerusalem at the center, are included in this sweep of faith as the Brethren see themselves at the heart of this world movement.

The following summarizes how the party "The Brothers of Jesus" saw themselves.

1. The group was made up of Jewish men. All the lines of address to the group underscore this point: *"There were dwelling in Jerusalem devout men from every nation under heaven"* (2:3). *"Men of Judea and all who dwell in Jerusalem"* (2:14); *"Men of Israel"* (2:22). These were the men who were attracted to the movement called "Brothers of Jesus."

   The group had multiple names. Sometimes it was called simply "Brethren." This, presumably, was in honor of the special relationship their leader had with Jesus. He may actually have been a blood brother; early historians of this period such as Josephus and Eusebius accord that birthright to him. On the other hand, he may have been designated "brother" because of the closeness to Jesus in thought, word, and deed that was attributed to him; certainly not all the others labelled "Brethren" were blood brothers of Jesus but were simply in the fellowship of the Brethren.

   Sometimes, as in Galatians 2:10 and possibly Matthew 5:3, the group was called "the poor." It was an honest designation. Being part of the Jesus movement in Jerusalem during the decades of the thirties through the fifties when feelings were high and outright persecution was an ever-present danger, they were cut off from their usual means of livelihood. As Luke described their plight, they had been hated, that is, put on probation by the leaders of the synagogues of Jerusalem; then excluded and reviled, that is, blacklisted by the community of believing Jews; then *"cast*

out by name as evil," that is, had their names read out
to members of the community, who were instructed
to have no further dealings with them (Lk 6:24). "No
further dealings" meant that no good Jew was to
patronize their business, buy their goods, sell their
products to them, employ their services, or marry
their daughters.

The whole infrastructure by which life in the community is sustained was cut off from them. The result
was they were poor. So it was by this name that a large
segment of the community was known. But just before
the Jewish rebellion of 70 C.E., remnants of the party
shuffled out of Jerusalem into the sands around Pella
in Jordan, and only fragments are recorded about them
in sources other than the New Testament. Still, as we
shall see, their importance continued through Hebrew-speaking congregations throughout the Roman
Empire, including those in Greece and Rome itself.

The congregations of these Brethren were governed by elders, as was the usual form of governance
of the Jewish synagogues of Jerusalem—when these
former Jews took the lead in the Jesus movement,
they carried with them their accustomed structures
of governance.

2. Echoes of God's establishing a new covenant with the
people of Israel reverberate through the event of Pentecost. In the Jewish thinking of this time, Pentecost
was seen as the feast of the law and the covenant, and
all the components for establishing a new covenant
were contained in the event recorded in Acts 2. Jerusalem is the Mt. Sinai of the New Testament; Jesus is
the new Moses through whom God acts. The spirit of
Jesus that descends upon them is the spirit promised
through the ages by the prophets—the spirit which,
as Joel proclaimed, will fall upon all flesh. This is the
promised day of the Lord. With this event, the new age
has begun. The men in that room that day understood

the event as the inauguration of God's new covenant with Israel through the death and resurrection, but especially through the ascension, of Jesus the Christ.

3. The speech attributed to Peter contains many of the primary doctrines of the Brethren movement. It began with the announcement that the age of fulfilment has dawned. The outpouring of the spirit of God upon all flesh, promised by the prophet Joel, has occurred. The day of the Lord has come.

This has taken place through one who was born of the lineage of David. In the message of the Brethren great emphasis was placed upon the Davidic descent of Jesus (Mt 1:1–22). What was only a secondary line of thinking in the other gospels and other New Testament writings was a primary doctrine to the Brethren. If they were to convince Jewish people that Jesus was Messiah, they had to convince them that he was of the line of David, for in Jewish thinking the messiah had to come through that family connection.

The actual ministry of Jesus was described in few words: *"mighty works, signs and wonders which God did through him"* (Acts 2:22). We need the complete gospels of our canon to enlarge this picture.

An unusual word was used to describe Jesus' relationship to God. *"Attested"* (2:22) meant "proclaimed in or appointed to office." A textual variant to this suggested that in the thinking of the Brethren Jesus was Messiah-elect during his earthly ministry (which may be the reason they made so little of the ministry) and entered his actual Messiahship only at his ascension. The Disciples of Peter saw Jesus as the suffering servant of God descended from the line of Joseph (Knohl, 2008, "The Messiah: Son of Joseph"). The Hellenists called him "Son of Humankind." The Apostles spoke of him as "the crucified and risen Lord." The Brethren called him "Messiah-designate" who upon his ascension assumed the role that God had designed for him.

Jesus was killed at the hands of lawless men. Here it is "lawless men" who kill Jesus and not "all Jews." The latter emphasis was reserved for the message of the Hellenists, who had far less regard for Jewish feelings than did the Brethren—the history of the world would have been far different had the church followed the message of the Brethren rather than that of the Hellenists.

But God raised Jesus from the dead to exalt him to God's right hand, so that through Christ the Holy Spirit might be poured upon all. This exalted Jesus Christ is the messianic head of the New Israel, composed of those who become part of the new covenant granted in this Pentecost after Jesus' crucifixion and resurrection.

The sign of the messianic age was the presence of the spirit of Jesus the Christ (the anointed). To have the spirit meant to have Jesus in his fullness present in one's life. Jesus, after his death, had a quality possessed by no one else in human history. Not only could those who knew him remember him. They also had the sense that the crucified Christ continued to respond to them and their needs. They needed forgiveness from sins; the crucified Christ provided it. They needed healing and wholeness; the risen Christ provided it. They needed direction for their lives and for their mission; the living Christ provided it. Jesus was not dead as others were dead. The risen Christ responded to his followers and their needs. They could respond to his words, his actions, his inner spirit. Such a response, said the Brethren, was the heart of the new age–the ascended Messiah recognized by these Christians remained with his people still.

The message culminated in an appeal for repentance. Repentance meant nothing less than the continual renewal of one's life through the influence of Christ's spirit. This placed the risen Messiah squarely at the center of one's life and practice. The law, the temple, the ritual baths, the circumcisions, the old covenant were fulfilled through him. *"Do not think that I have come to abolish the law and the prophets,"* the Brothers understood Christ, the anointed Messiah, to say. *"I have come not to abolish but to fulfill"* (Mt 5:17). To those who turn to the spirit of Christ, renewal will surely come.

The character of this party of James is further delineated by a short passage that seems to intrude on the story. When the sound came from heaven like the rush of a mighty wind and the tongues of fire appeared on each one and they began to speak in other tongues, some who saw it mocked by saying, *"They are filled with new wine"* (2:13). The use of this "new wine" (or "sweet wine" as a more accurate translation put it) was related to the vows taken by a Nazarite. Nazarites were men who had sworn total fidelity to the Lord God of Israel, wore their hair long as a sign of their vow and refrained from drinking the fermented wines that were the customary fare of Jewish people. "Sweet wine," however, was permissible to a Nazarite. This was a wine from the preceding year's vintage and was only lightly fermented.

The significance of this lay in a description of James, the brother, given by the church historian Eusebius. Eusebius (*Church History* 11, 23, 4–18) said that James was a Nazarite. "He was holy from his mother's womb. He did not drink wine and strong drink, nor did he eat meat. No razor touched his head. He did not anoint himself with oil, and he did not frequent the baths.... He wore nothing of wool but only linen. He used to go to the temple alone and kneel and pray for forgiveness for the people, so that his knees became hard as a camel's because of his constant kneeling, worshiping God and praying for forgiveness for the people." If the party took on the character of its leader, it was then a party of stringent rules, fervent in prayer, holding hard to those Jewish things that Jesus had fulfilled by his coming.

As Jewish followers of Jesus they tried to remain good Jews as well as become good Christians. They worshipped in the Temple, read the Bible in Hebrew, conducted their services in the same sacred language, paid the temple tax, practiced the food laws of Judaism, circumcised their male infants, and performed rites prescribed by their law. The Brothers of Jesus followed what they thought to be the example of their older brother and practiced the Christian faith in the manner of good Jews.

The worship services of this group are described in a summary section: *"They devoted themselves to the teaching and fellowship, to the breaking of bread and the prayers"* (Acts 2:42). Their services of house worship originally had supplemented their worship in the synagogues and at the temple. Later the house service became the norm for their worship and praise of God.

The service began by giving attention to the teaching of Jesus as it had been delivered to them. This was followed by table fellowship as the group shared a meal together. At the close of the meal came the sacred ritual. The bread was torn, as the body of Jesus had been torn, and all shared in it. This was followed by the prayers, probably modeled on the Jewish prayers over the cup or upon the Lord's prayer; Jesus' words in Luke (11:1–4, *"Lord, teach us to pray, as John taught his disciples,"* followed by Jesus' response, *"Father, hallowed be thy name")* could well have been used for direction.

ii

Many of the theological motifs of the Brethren party resonate through the Gospel of Matthew. Matthew took the basic outline that Mark gave to a Gospel and employed it in his own book. He expanded upon it, so much so that scholars formerly thought that Mark was an abridgement of Matthew rather than an independent writing. The deeper one penetrates into Matthew, the clearer it is that this Gospel had themes that reflected the concerns of the Brothers of Jesus.

The primary theme of the book was its emphasis upon "righteousness." This can be defined as "getting on right terms with God, neighbor, self, and the world around through Jesus Christ." The theme was set out in the scene of Jesus' baptism. John the Baptizer wanted to know why Jesus had come to him to be baptized and Jesus replied, *"In order to fulfill all righteousness"* (Mt 3:15). The theme came to high expression in the Sermon on the Mount: *"Seek first the kingdom of God and its righteousness"* (Mt 6:33). The last parable of Jesus given in the Gospel brought the theme to a fitting conclusion. The king, seated on his throne, was about to make his judgments on the validity of human lives. The judgments were made solely on the basis of whether the person had acted righteously: *"For I was hungry and you gave me food, I was thirsty and you gave me drink, I was a stranger and you welcomed me, I was naked and you clothed me, I was sick and you visited me, I was in prison and you came to me"* (Mt 25:35–36). The righteous person is the one who does these things.

There seems also to be an internal organization in this Gospel that is related to the five books of the Law of Moses. Scholars have isolated five major sections, which they call "books," inside this one book:

The Book of Discipleship, chapters 3 through 7
The Book of Apostleship, chapters 8 through 10
The Book of the Mystery, chapters 11 through 13
The Book of the Church, chapters 14 through 18
The Book of the Future, chapters 19 through 25

Each section begins with narrative material and ends with teaching material. Since this teaching material was quite different and much more extensive than that of Mark's Gospel, we are indebted to Matthew for having preserved it.

To the body of this text two things were added: the passion story at the end, with additional accounts of the resurrection of Jesus, and a prologue at the beginning.

The passion narrative was so similar to Mark's that we need not comment on it. The prologue, though, was unique. This prologue—our contemporary Christmas story—was constructed around Old Testament passages that Matthew found pertinent to Jesus. Much of it appears to have been composed in Aramaic, the language of the Brothers, then translated into the familiar Greek of Matthew's Gospel. In his selection of text and event the author of Matthew went further than Mark in pointing out how Jesus had recapitulated in his own person the Old Testament experience.

Matthew began with a genealogy tracing Jesus' lineage back to Abraham, neatly schematizing it as fourteen generations from Abraham to David, fourteen generations from David to the deportation into Babylon, and fourteen generations from then until the Jesus' birth. "Fourteen" is "twice seven" and "seven" is the perfect number, its components being "three," the number for heaven, and "four," the number for earth. Seven is the perfection of everything in heaven and on earth and twice seven is infinitely better than that—a very neat scheme Matthew devised!

In the stories of Jesus' birth, Matthew worked out a five-fold pattern, beginning with using five Old Testament passages as the basis for his narrative. He told how Jesus was born of a virgin; had his nativity in the favored city of Bethlehem, the home of David; was taken into Egypt as an infant so that God may be said to have drawn his son from Egypt; fulfilled the prophecy of the wailing and loud lamentation of Judah as the infants of Bethlehem were slain by Herod; and went to Nazareth that he might be called a Nazarene.

Matthew also exhibits a concern with problems of the organization of the church and its congregations. In chapters 14 through 18 especially, but with hints of it elsewhere as well, Matthew turned to questions about worship, theology, ethics, and leadership which did not appear in Mark.

This interest parallels a similar movement within the Judaism of Matthew's time. When the war over Jerusalem between Jews and Romans ended with the destruction of Jerusalem in 70 C.E., rabbinic leaders settled near the town of Jamnia (called in Hebrew "Yavneh") on the Mediterranean coast and began to organize into meaningful patterns the oral tradition of Judaism and to codify the Jewish laws and Scriptures. Matthew showed a similar interest arising from a similar situation and time, and this would indicate that this writer and his congregation were in contact with Jewish movements of the day.

This has led scholars to suppose that Matthew was writing his Gospel for a Christian congregation composed largely of Jewish people and was attempting to interpret Christ to people who were deeply nurtured in the Old Testament and especially the five books of the Law. Since this gospel showed knowledge of the catastrophe that befell the Holy City in 70 C.E. and indicated much interest in the organizational problems faced by the Christian congregations after this event, Matthew was probably composed in its entirety in the late seventies or early eighties of the first century of the common era.

iii

Traces of their theology also turn up in the strangest place, namely, in the letters of their rival, Paul. One comes from Paul's letter to the Galatians, a group of congregations in the areas of Pamphylia and Lyaconia, notably Perga, Derbe, and Lystra. Paul wrote the letter to the churches after he had completed his ministry with them. The letter was written as Paul was on the way to the important meeting called the Council of Jerusalem, where he hoped to resolve issues that had arisen in his ministry in Galatia. In the letter Paul incorporated a short passage that told of the coming of Jesus as Christ and the impact of his life and work. This passage turns out to be the earliest meditation on the meaning of Christ's coming that we have in the New Testament. Translated directly from the Greek of Paul's letter, the statement reads:

And when came the fulness of the time
Sent forth God his son
   born from a woman
   born under law
so that those under law might be redeemed
so that the adoption as sons we might receive.
   And because we are sons

*Sent forth God the spirit of his son into our hearts crying,
    Abba, Father,
  so that no longer am I a slave but a son
and if a son, also an heir through God. (Gal 4:4–7)*

This creed most likely emerged from the Aramaic-speaking churches in the early Jesus movement. They had worked out their own creeds and confessions, and these few verses constituted one of them. Paul incorporated it into his letter to the Galatian congregations in order to show his respect for them and their style of Christian life.

The word order of the sentences in the creed points to this conclusion. Paul, who was more than capable of writing a grammatically correct Greek sentence, has here placed the verb at the beginning of the sentence, a natural thing to do if the translator was translating directly from another language like Aramaic which regularly has the verb in the first position. The balance within the statement also breathes the atmosphere of the Aramaic-speaking churches. The statement was composed in the parallel form familiar in Hebrew poetry and the psalms, *"sent forth God his son,...sent forth God the spirit of his son..."* Here, also, as frequently in the New Testament, the Aramaic name for father was given, a word directly understood by the churches in Judea and Galilee but needing the translation Paul supplied if it was to be intelligible to the churches in Galatia.

The theology of this passage is also that of a Torah-observant congregation. The son whom God sent was born from a woman, that is, was born to lead a fully human life under conditions like those of any other man born of a woman. He was also born under the law, taking upon himself the cultural, religious, and legal traditions that all Jewish people shared. But the son (neither "Jesus" nor "Christ" is used in this formula, another indication that Paul did not formulate it, for he used those two terms freely in setting out his own theology) came to redeem those under the law; to restore to the lost and defenseless ones all the benefits of their inheritance; and to receive the orphan into the father's home. As a sign of these things, each can call God by the name Jesus had given God, *"Abba, Father."* Indeed, being able to name God as "Father" is a sure sign of one's inclusion in the family of God.

But no one does this unaided. This occurs only when God has sent the spirit of his son into our hearts. These converts to the Jesus movement, who considered themselves to be living at the decisive point of all history when God has prepared all things properly, when, as they said, *"the fulness of time had come,"* they had been recipients of the two greatest gifts of all: God had sent forth his son so that we might receive adoption into God's family; and God had sent forth the spirit of his son into our hearts so that with Christ we might cry out to God, *"Abba, father."*

In the Letter to the Romans, a similar event occurs. The heart of Paul's greeting to the church in Rome is found in verses three and four of chapter one: *"The gospel concerning his Son, who was descended from David according to the flesh and was designated Son of God in power according to the Spirit of holiness by his resurrection from the dead, Jesus Christ our Lord."* This also appears to be a creedal statement drawn from the Jewish Christian party of the Jesus movement, which, up to now, has been the main opponent within the Christian faith to the kind of ministry that Paul conducted.

"Descended from David...designated Son of God in power" are the key phrases. Jewish Christians had celebrated the fact that Jesus was in the line of David, the just and pious king whom God chose through Samuel and whose successor all Judaism awaited. Jesus was that successor, this creed asserted. He was *"designated Son of God in power"* when he rose from the dead. These Jewish Christians did not think that Jesus was the Messiah until he had risen from the dead. The resurrection was, according to this party of Christians, the designation of Jesus as the Son of God in power.

As important as the words of the creed is its placement at the very beginning of his letter to the Romans. In this letter

Paul was attempting to reconcile the Gentile members of the church in Rome with those Jewish members who had been expelled from Rome by an edict of the Emperor Claudius and with his recent death were now returning to the Imperial City. By his emphasis on this creed, he is expressing his personal willingness to reconcile with those Jewish Christians who had fought against him so bitterly in Syria, Galatia, and Greece and who continued to oppose him right up to the Council of Jerusalem just a few years before. In this letter Paul will argue for the primacy of the Jews who provided the teachings, the prophecies, and the traditions from which Jesus came. It was a generous act on Paul's part to put this passage at the very beginning of his letter.

iv

The party of the Brethren had firm control of the Christian movement from about 44 C.E. (the demise of the "Peter-party") until about 62. The strength that the Brethren party assumed is indicated in significant portions of Acts. Brethren formed one of the parties of the church in Lystra and Iconium (16:2), as well as in Thessalonika (17:5–9). They seemed especially strong in Ephesus, for that church governed itself with elders according to the Jewish practice. A group of them wrote to the church in Corinth to receive Apollos who wanted to come to Corinth to work (18:24–28). The party in Corinth known as "the Christ party" (1 Cor 1:12) may have been the local Brethren group in Corinth, because it appears to have been the most conservative of the parties in the Corinthian fellowship.They had also reached Rome early, and continued to influence the life and faith of the church there.

The Brethren as a party show up many times in the closing chapters of Acts. At Ptolemais, Paul stayed with "Brethren" for one day (Acts 21:7), and when he arrived in Jerusalem on that journey, the Brethren, including James and the elders, greeted him gladly (21:17–18). The account of Paul's subsequent arrest and trial (21:17–24:27 and possibly all of Acts to 26:32) seems to have been presented from the perspective of the Brethren. Later, when Paul arrived in Rome, the Brethren from the Roman church came out to meet him and reported to him that no ill word concerning him had come from the Brethren in Judea, either by letter or by word of mouth (28:11–22). Following the thesis that set up this narrative, the party of the Brethren seem more powerful at the end of the story than at its beginning.

The last days of James, leader of the Brethren in Jerusalem, are recounted to us not in Scripture but in the history of the Jewish people called *The Antiquities of the Jews* written by Josephus. This Jewish nobleman turned Roman general wrote that in the interval between the death of the governor Festus and the coming of his successor Albinus (the date being 62 C.E.), Ananos the high priest took advantage of the lack of a Roman governor in the area. He called a meeting of the Sanhedrin and brought James and some others before them. Charging them with transgressing the law, he handed them over to be stoned to death (*Antiquities* 20:200). Eusebius, the church historian, added that as James was being stoned, he prayed, "I beseech thee, Lord God and Father, forgive them, for they do not know what they are doing." As he was saying this, a certain laundryman took the club by which he beat the clothes and struck James on the head until he died (*Church History II*, 23:4–18).

The Brethren in Jerusalem did not long outlast their leader. At the death of James, the group chose Simeon, a relative of the deceased leader, to take his place. As the rumors of war began to close around them in the events that led up to the outbreak of fighting about 66 C.E., the Jerusalem Brethren made a decision to leave the city and relocate across the Jordan in a city called Pella. Remnants of the group, called Ebionites after the Hebrew word for "the poor," remained in the area around Pella for more than two centuries. A tiny band of the Poor made their way to Egypt seeking safety. A small portion of the group remained in Jerusalem during the

Jewish rebellions of 70 and 132 C.E. and became the basis for the church that Helena, mother of the Emperor Constantine, found when she made her pilgrimage to the Holy Land in the mid-fourth century. But to trace this later history takes us beyond the time limit set for our study.

V

At this point, we can continue to fill in the thirteen cells of the summary table. This party was called together in the spirit of the Pentecost, dating to when it believed Jesus ascended into heaven and became the promised Messiah to Israel. Its governance in synagogues was similar to what was found in Jewish synagogues; each synagogue was governed by the elders of the local entity. Only men, not women, were considered to be members of a synagogue. The composition of the party, then, was Jewish men and their families with traditional male-dominance in the family.

Their mission and target audience were initially the synagogues in Jerusalem, but soon thereafter the target became urban-based Hebrew-speaking synagogues throughout the Roman world. Their major places of worship were the Temple, synagogues, and, especially where traditional Jewish synagogues had shut them out, even house churches. As practicing Jews, they closely adhered to circumcision, food, and marriage laws.

As expressed in their writings, Matthew, James, Jude, and Revelation, they understood themselves theologically as being part of the new, or, more accurately, renewed covenant between God and Israel, between God the Father and his "families." This revelation was both generated and reinforced by the life and resurrection of Jesus. Their primary ethical principles focused on being "right" with God the Father, and seeking "his righteousness," in terms of caring for the poor (which many of them, literally, had become) and those unable to care for themselves such as those in prison (and some of them were also in prison).

Table 3. The Brethren and Their Heritage on Thirteen Major Issues.

Parties	The Twelve Disciples	Brethren	Hellenists	Apostles
Beginning Event	Jesus's call in Galilee	Coming of the Spirit at Pentecost		
Governance	Cephas; The Twelve, the Assembly of 70	James; Elders		
Mission Targets	Synagogues in Galilee, Gaza	Hebrew-speaking synagogues		
Composition of Party	Jewish men in leadership, some women	Jewish men and their families		
Places of Worship	Temple, synagogues, house churches	Temple, synagogues, house churches		
Circumcision	Jewish men and proselytes before the Jerusalem Conference; only Jewish men after	Jewish men		
Food Laws	Kept, then did not	Kept all kosher laws		
Marriage Laws	Married Jewish women	Married Jewish women		
Theological Self-Understanding	Successor to Israel	Covenant renewed		
Role of Jesus	Servant of God	Designated as Messiah at death, Son of David		

Parties	The Twelve Disciples	Brethren	Hellenists	Apostles
Primary Ethical Principle	"Take up cross, follow me"	"Seek God's righteousness"		
Writings	Mark 1st Peter	Matthew James Jude Revelation		
Terminating Event	Death of leaders under Herod Agrippa	Death of James & leaders, Jewish war 66–79 C.E.		–

Terminating events of the initial congregation(s) in Jerusalem, prior to the Jewish War of 66–70 C.E. from which they separated themselves, happened when they moved across the Jordan to Pella. Still, Hebrew-speaking Christian congregations in the diaspora competed with Greek-speaking congregations and very slowly faded away once the latter became dominant after about 100 C.E.

CHAPTER 4

The Hellenists

There is an odd sense of incompleteness, of lack of connection, in the story in Mark's Gospel (10:17–22) traditionally called "The Story of the Rich Young Ruler." Jesus was on his way to Jerusalem for his final confrontation with the authorities there, when this man knelt before him with his question, *"What must I do to inherit eternal life?"* Jesus recites six of the commandments to him, and the man surprises Jesus by saying that he has kept all these things since his youth. *"One thing you lack,"* replied Jesus. *"Go, sell all you have, and give it to the poor, and you will have treasure in heaven. And come, follow me."* At this, wrote Mark, the man's countenance fell, and he went away sorrowful. For he had great possessions.

The oddness of the story lies in two lines. *"What must I do to inherit eternal life?"* the man asked. Nowhere else in the gospels of Mark, Matthew, and Luke (called the synoptic gospels because of their repetition of basically the same stories) is the concept "eternal life" used. Of no one else in these gospels is it said that *"Jesus, looking on him, loved him"* (10:21). How do we account for these unusual statements?

Strange to the synoptics, this concept of eternal life is the centerpiece of the Gospel of John. *"God so loved the world that he sent his only son, that whoever believes on him shall have eternal life." "I am the resurrection and the life." "This is eternal life, to know God and Jesus Christ whom he has sent"* (Jn 3:16; 11:25; 17:3). Reflection also tells us that the central figure of the Gospel of John, other than Jesus, is a man known as "the disciple whom Jesus loved."

This person does not arrive in John's gospel story until Jesus has drawn close to Jerusalem for that final confrontation. We see him first in a message that his sisters, Mary and Martha, send to Jesus: *"Lord, he whom you love is ill"* (Jn 11:2). This relationship is amplified by a remark added by the evangelist: *"Now Jesus loved Martha and her sister and Lazarus"* (Jn 11:5). In a story that takes a whole chapter in the gospel to tell, Lazarus dies, and Jesus calls him forth from the dead. *"I am the resurrection and the life,"* Jesus announces, and he calls out, *"Lazarus, come out."* And the dead man emerges from his tomb (Jn 11:25–44).

The Beloved Disciple appears six other times in the narrative of John. He is the one who has the choice spot at the last supper of Jesus with his disciples; he is *"lying close to the breast of Jesus"* (13:23). Most likely he is the *"other disciple known to the high priest"* who with Simon Peter enters the court of the high priest and hears the interrogation of Jesus by the high priest (18:15–24). He could have also been present at Pilate's questioning of Jesus at the praetorium. He is surely present at Jesus' crucifixion (19:26–27), because it is in this excruciating moment that Jesus bequeaths the care of his mother to this disciple. He is the first man to reach the tomb of Jesus on the morning of resurrection (20:3–9) and the first to *"see and believe."* He is also in Galilee when Jesus reveals himself once more by the Sea of Tiberius (21:20–23).

He is also the one of whom it is said, *"This is the disciple who is bearing witness to these things, and who has written these things, and we know that his testimony is true"* (21:24). In other words, what is written in the Gospel of John is attributed to him. It is on the basis of his testimony that the unique witness of this gospel stands or falls.

Can we trust the account of this witness to be an authentic retelling of the gospel story? Many scholars throughout the ages have said "No. This gospel is a theological reflection on the meaning of Jesus Christ, but it bears little historical accuracy." C. H. Dodd, in his *Historical Tradition in the Fourth Gospel*, challenges the idea. He says, instead, that "behind the Fourth Gospel lies an ancient tradition independent of the other gospels, and meriting serious consideration as a contribution to our knowledge of the historical facts concerning Jesus Christ"(423). He adds (426) "The basic tradition on which the evangelist is working was shaped in a Jewish-Christian environment still in touch with the synagogue, in Palestine, at a relatively early date, at any rate before the rebellion of c.e. 66)." It is within this Jewish-Christian environment, still in touch with the synagogue, in Palestine and beyond, at a relatively early date, related to the Fourth Gospel and its Letters, that we locate the theology and practice of the Hellenist movement. Its theology is clear from the Gospel of John: *"God so loved the world that he sent his son"* (3:16). Its ethic is also clear: *"Love one another as I have loved you"* (13:34).

ii

In contradiction to both the theology and the ethic of the Hellenists, they engineered a split in the Jesus movement between the Hellenists and the Hebrews. This rupture occurred barely a year after the resurrection of Jesus had energized the disciples to begin their mission for Christ. But the tensions that caused the division had been building for centuries.

The ostensible reason for the rift was the complaint by the Hellenists that their widows were not receiving a fair share of the daily distribution. The actual reason centered on the ethnic and religious tensions that had divided Judaism for centuries before.

When the Twelve and their followers had come up to Jerusalem with Jesus from Galilee for the feast of Passover in the year that Jesus died, they were barely aware that Jesus had previously assembled another group of followers in Jerusalem and Judea. They had thought that they were Jesus' only real followers, but this was not so. Jesus' own brothers had become followers of his (see Acts 1:14), though the Disciples earlier had not regarded them as such. The Disciples had pictured Jesus as turning his back on his mother and brothers when they attempted to follow him, and declaring that others, those who did the will of God, were his true family (Mk 3:31–35 and parallels). The brothers had already begun to attract to the Jesus movement other persons from the Hebrew-speaking synagogues who were, like Jesus and themselves, Jews of standing who had been circumcised and who believed that Jesus, like themselves, was purely Jewish in his actions.

These the Galilean Disciples could tolerate. It was the Hellenists who attracted to the movement men like Philip who had come down from Bethsaida in Galilee to settle in Jerusalem, and John, and that disputatious Stephen, whom they had trouble accepting.

The word *Hellenist*, as it is used here, needs definition. Hellenists were Jews, some born and bred into Judaism and some from families that had long ago been proselytized into the faith. These people spoke only Greek and could hardly understand either the Hebrew of the Scriptures used in the synagogues or the Aramaic that most Hebrew Jews spoke at home and on the street. Some Hellenists had been in Judea for centuries. The earliest records about them came from the reign of Ptolemy II, who had ruled in Judea from 285 to 246 B.C.E. They used Greek in their synagogues. This meant that their Scripture was not the sacred Hebrew text but was a translation from the Hebrew, called the Septuagint, which had been made in Alexandria, Egypt, about the time of Ptolemy II. Named for the seventy scholars who reputedly worked on the translation ("Septuagint" means "seventy" in Greek and the symbol for this translation today is the Latin number for seventy, LXX), it was considered by the Hellenists to be as divinely inspired as the Hebrew Bible itself, and even some of the Hebrews reluctantly assigned this authority to it. In their synagogues Hellenists conducted not only their readings but also their prayers in Greek.

As if the language problem were not enough, many Hellenists, especially those who lived in cities far from Jerusalem, had begun to affect a cultural superiority toward Hebrew- and Aramaic-speaking Jews. The history of the word "Hellenist" indicates the tension. Coming from the Greek word "'ellenizo," it originally meant "to speak Greek" and had specifically referred to those who used the Greek language correctly and did not introduce barbarisms or colloquialisms into the language. Later, it began to designate those who adopted Greek manners and ways of life, who, though coming from other families and nations, had claimed to be Greek in thought, word, and deed. Hellenists, especially those who lived away from Jerusalem, retraced in their own attitudes and actions the history of the word.

These diaspora Hellenists found it easy to take on Greek ways and airs. Because they had Greek-speaking friends outside their synagogues, they liked to rub elbows with them both personally and professionally. They did not keep the food laws of Judaism with the same rigor that the Hebrews did. It would hurt their social life and business dealings to do so, and they found reasons in the Scriptures as to why it was not necessary to be stringent about these rules. They permitted the women in their synagogues greater freedom of association than the Hebrews tended to do. Greek and Roman women took a leading role in the festive dinners of the pagan temples, and their Jewish female counterparts among the Hellenists insisted that those positions be open to them as well. Some Hellenists permitted intermarriage between Greek-speaking pagans and Greek-speaking Jews, and some not only permitted it but encouraged it. Nicolaus, the proselyte from Antioch who became one of the Seven, was one church leader who did this, and this issue became critical at the Jerusalem Council that was still to come.

These Jews of the diaspora even began to claim that they had a more pure and more legitimate comprehension of Old Testament faith than did their Judean counterparts. This especially concerned the place the temple and its sacrificial system held in the faith. They flatly asserted that neither of these was necessary for the practice of true Jewish faith. Part of their position, undoubtedly, was developed from their geography. When Jewish families lived in Italy, Alexandria, Asia, Cyrene, or Cilicia, they could not worship in the temple as regularly as could the Jews resident in Jerusalem. So they began to make a virtue of necessity. They insisted that temple worship and animal sacrifice were not fundamental to the worship of the God Yahweh, and they searched their Scriptures for verses and texts to prove it. From the point of view of those who spoke Hebrew in their synagogues, who adhered strictly to what they considered to be the traditional ways of life, and who worshipped regularly in the temple, these Hellenists from the outlands had an irritating way of looking down their noses at the Hebrews.

But two could play the game of cultural superiority, and Hebrews returned Hellenists' derogations. More than any other people of the time, Jews who considered themselves truly Jewish were not inclined to learn and speak foreign languages and were certainly not prepared to take on foreign ways. Further, about two centuries earlier the Jews of Judea had fought a long and bitter war for independence from a Greek-speaking opponent who had tried to introduce Greek culture into Judea. The memory of this struggle burned savagely within them. Led by the Hasmoneans, a family of priests and Jewish patriots whose sire and spiritual leader was Simon Maccabaeus, they had fought brilliantly and zealously against the power of the Seleucid dynasty in Syria, whose capital city was Antioch and whose leaders were the family of Antiochus.

The war had begun in 167 B.C.E. with a report that Antiochus Epiphanes IV, the contemporary Seleucid ruler, had sacrificed a pig on the altar at Jerusalem. While this so-called "abomination of desolation" was no more true than most war-born rumors, it inflamed the Jews to do battle against their Greek-speaking rulers. The conflict turned out to be not so much a struggle against a particular enemy as it was against the way of life represented by Greek language and culture. The fighting had dragged on for over a century and had only ended when Rome placed the governance of Judea into the hands of Herod and his family, a family who themselves had dubious Jewish roots since they were imported from the Arabian desert to rule and had only converted to Judaism when Augustus Caesar had made them rulers over his newly formed province of Judea. It is no wonder that most Hebrews could scarcely tolerate the Hellenists.

Another ingredient to the already boiling pot was that the Hellenists who lived in Jerusalem were as zealous for the Judaism they practiced as were the Hebrews in Jerusalem for the faith as they conducted it. A sizable number of Greek-speaking Jews had settled permanently in the Holy City, so many that at least three, and possibly more, Hellenist synagogues had been organized in Jerusalem by the time of Jesus (Acts 6:9). These conditions formed a core of Hebrew-speaking synagogues certain their practice of Judaism was prescribed in the Hebrew Scriptures arrayed against an Hellenistic Judaism whose adherents lived in Jerusalem because they wanted to be in the center where the faith was purely practised and who looked down on the way Torah-observant Jews in Jerusalem pursued the faith. Clearly, the elements for an explosion over ethnic and cultural differences were present, even among the followers of Jesus, which included both Hellenists and Hebrews.

iii

The precipitating issue turned out to be "the daily distribution" to the widows (Acts 6:1). It referred to the practice of Jewish synagogues by which they gave direct aid to the widows of members of their synagogue. Jewish women had very little legal and economic protection when their husbands died. They and their children could return to their own families, if their father or a brother-in-law were affluent enough to take them in. Or they could fall back on the dowry they had brought with them to the marriage, the amount of money their family had provided as their insurance policy against their husband's early death. Frequently neither of these alternatives was able to provide the necessary care for a widow and her children. So the synagogues took on themselves the care of these otherwise indigent families and provided them with food and other necessities of life.

When the Peters, Jameses, Philips, and Stephens left the Jewish synagogues to form their own communities of worship, they took with them the practice of "daily distribution" to the widows. But was the distribution equal? The Hellenists thought not. They compiled complaints from their widows that they were being short-changed in the distribution. The leaders of the Hellenist wing of the movement took their complaints to the Hebrew leaders and asked for resolution of the matter.

The Twelve, as active leaders of these congregations, called an assembly of all the Disciples to deal with the problem. The minutes taken at this open assembly are only skimpily reported in Acts (6:2–6). But what we are told permits us to reconstruct the meeting along the following lines.

The Twelve gave the impression that they did not want to be bothered by a matter as inconsequential as this. Preaching was their calling, and they did not want their mission cluttered with unnecessary administrative details. Their solution was to choose *"seven men of good repute, full of the Spirit and of wisdom, whom we will appoint to the duty"* of seeing to the distribution for the widows (Acts 6:3). Seven were chosen. Since all their names were Greek, they presumably came from the Hellenist side of the dispute. They were set aside for their office by prayer and the laying on of hands (6:6).

The Seven did not confine their work to the distribution for widows. Immediately, they too engaged in preaching and in producing signs and wonders among the people (6:8). The number of Disciples in Jerusalem multiplied (6:7).

But Stephen was not content with merely preaching. He began to debate issues of faith with his Hebrew neighbors. The debate focused on the place of the temple and of the law in Hellenist life or, as it was put, *"This man never ceases to speak words against this holy place and the law. We have heard him say that this Jesus of Nazareth will destroy (the temple) and will change the customs which Moses delivered to us"* (Acts 6:13–14). Stephen's position, and that of the Christian Hellenists, is summarized in chapter seven of Acts.

1. These Hellenists did not revere the temple as the dwelling place of God. Stephen declared that Jewish forebears in the wilderness had not worshipped in a temple but in the tent of witness (7:44). He insisted that it was not the revered David who built the temple but the less well regarded Solomon (7:45–47). He concluded by stating dogmatically that *"The Most High does not dwell in houses made with hands"* but that *"Heaven is (God's) throne and earth (God's) footstool"* (7:48–49).

2. He pointed out that the history of the People of God was that of fighting against God's holy will. The people had not accepted Moses as their leader but had worshipped the calf of Moloch and the star of Rephan (7:17–43). They had refused to hear the prophets and instead had killed them. Even his present hearers he characterized as *"stiff-necked people, uncircumcised in heart and ears, who resisted the Holy Spirit"* as did their forebears who had killed the prophets, and the present company who had killed the Christ (7:51–53).

3. As to the law, that most precious possession of Judaism, it also was suspect in Stephen's eyes. It had not been bestowed upon them by God as the Jews believed, said Stephen. It had been given to them by an intermediate hand, by angels instead of by God (7:53). Yet, even though it was of secondary origin

and therefore not a means of coming into contact directly with God, even that derivative law they did not keep. They were a renegade bunch.

4. There was no call for repentance in the Hellenists' message. Their opponents were lost in their sins and in the sins of their forebears.

5. Their belief in Jesus was built around the concept of Jesus as the Son of Humankind. This article of faith remained largely undefined in the book of Acts. Our only hint to its meaning in Acts is that it pictured Jesus as standing at the right hand of God (7:55) when God's heavenly court was in session and defending his faithful Disciples against the charges laid against them by their enemies.

iv

Such an attack on the sacred institutions of Judaism could not go unnoticed. What followed in Acts (7:55–60) is one of the most poignant scenes in Scripture. The account of the trial and death of Stephen coincided point by point with the account of the trial and death of Jesus. The nuances that come in comparing the two trials give meaning to the martyrdom of Stephen.

Like Jesus, Stephen was tried by the council of Jerusalem, the scribes and elders of the Sanhedrin. His trial, like that of Jesus, was a quick and violent affair. Hardly had Stephen completed his defence when his accusers cried with a loud voice, rushed together upon him, conveyed him out of the city, and commenced to stone him.

While this trial was moving toward its fateful conclusion, Stephen was aware that another trial was simultaneously taking place, this one in heaven. The verdict of heaven was different from the verdict of earth. Stephen saw Jesus, the Son of Humankind, standing in the holy throne room of God, pleading his case before the Almighty Judge. The voice of Jesus, Son of Humankind, the attorney for the defence, prevailed, and Stephen was declared innocent by God, the Holy Judge.

The death of Stephen recapitulated the death of Jesus as it was told by Luke, who, most scholars agree, wrote both the Gospel bearing his name and the Acts of the Apostles that followed it. The victims' garments were at the center of both stories. While Jesus died, his garments were divided by the execution detail. While Stephen died, the garments of his executioners were protected by a young man named Saul. When Jesus was suffering on the cross, he said (Lk 23:34), *"Father, forgive them, for they know not what they do."* When Stephen was feeling the first stones crash upon his back and neck, he cried, *"Lord, do not hold this sin against them"* (Acts 7:60). As Jesus died, he cried with a loud voice, *"Father, into thy hands I commit my spirit"* (Lk 23:46). As Stephen died, he prayed, *"Lord Jesus, receive my spirit."* In the Hellenist Stephen, the Jesus movement had its first martyr. His death was seen as being truly in the spirit of Christ's.

What happened next was catastrophic. A great persecution arose against the congregations of the Jesus movement in Jerusalem, and members of both parties, both Hellenists and Hebrew-speakers, were scattered throughout the regions of Judea and Samaria (8:1). Some, probably Hellenists (we are following a Hellenist document within Acts) ranged north into Phoenicia, crossed the sea to the island of Cyprus, and journeyed on to Antioch in Syria (11:20–21). Everywhere they went they spoke in the synagogues of the Torah-observant Jews about Jesus Christ. But when they came to Antioch, they began also to speak to Greeks, and a great number of these turned to Jesus as the Christ. Having faced catastrophe, the Christians (the name was first used in Antioch as a term of contempt) turned it into opportunity. Soon, as the Holy Spirit had promised at the beginning (Acts 1:8), the word of Jesus Christ had spread beyond Jerusalem into Judea and Samaria and to the ends of the earth.

V

The member of the Seven who took the lead in many of these new ministries was Philip. His missionary efforts are recounted more fully in Acts than are those of any other of the original Seven.

Philip went first to a city in Samaria (8:4), where he proclaimed Christ to the Samaritans. His proclamation had a hearing among the people. Signs broke out. Unclean spirits came out of those who were possessed, and many paralyzed and lame persons were healed (8:7). Word went back to Jerusalem that Philip's ministry was effective among the Samaritans, and those who had remained in Jerusalem rejoiced.

A second opportunity presented itself to Philip (8:26–40). By divine direction, Philip went south to the Gaza Road (the road on the narrow strip of fertile land connecting Judea to the north and Egypt to the south) and met a high official from the court of Candace, the queen of Ethiopia. This Ethiopian was in charge of finances for the kingdom and had been in Jerusalem on the queen's business. There he had picked up a scroll from the prophet Isaiah. As he was seated in his chariot puzzling over this scroll, Philip joined him to ask if he understood what he was reading. He did not, he admitted, so Philip proceeded to interpret it for him. The passage before him spoke of one who, like a sheep, was led to slaughter. Philip told how this referred to Jesus of Nazareth and of the good news that had come to the world through him. So impressed was the Ethiopian official that he asked to be part of the movement and under Philip's hand was baptized. The Ethiopian official sped off toward home rejoicing.

These two accounts of Philip's short mission journey are among the most important in Scripture. We wish that we knew a great deal more about their details.

The first indicated a mission by members of the Jesus movement into Samaria. Though little is recorded in Scripture of this mission, the Gospel of John (4:4–42) tells of a short encounter Jesus had with Samaritans, beginning with the woman at the well of Sychar and resulting in the state-ment that *"Many Samaritans came to Jesus and remained with him two days."* In this encounter Jesus had said, *"The fields are ripe for the harvest, but the saying is true that one sows and another reaps. I sent you to reap that for which you did not labor."* Apparently John's Gospel reminded his hearers that sometime earlier a mission had begun in Samaria and that later, when some of them went to Samaria, they would discover that others from the Jesus movement had already labored there. Philip's short ministry in Samaria had initi-ated work in Christ's name that the author of John's Gospel hoped would result in evangelization of that territory alien to Jews and Christians alike.

The second story told of the entrance of the gospel into Egypt. The Ethiopian, in returning to his own land, had to travel through Egypt up the Nile Valley to his kingdom in the south. Short as the story is, it contains the first record of the incursion of the gospel ("good news") of Jesus the Christ into Egypt. When hints dropped into the stories of the Hellenists are related to the little that is known of Chris-tian congregations in Egypt, the implications are huge, for they begin to tie the ministry of the Seven to the church in Egypt.

Quotations from the Scripture given in Stephen's speech are not taken from the Hebrew Bible but from the Septuagint, the Scripture of Egypt and Alexandria. The Epistle of Barna-bas, which was written in Alexandria around 118 C.E., closely resembled the position that Stephen had outlined, so the in-fluence of this theology had a long-lasting effect in Egypt. Philo of Alexandria supported Stephen's version of Scripture that God came to Abraham before Abraham lived in Haran (Acts 7:2), as opposed to the official Hebrew account that God had visited Abraham only after he had moved to Ha-ran. Stephen had described in some detail the comparisons and contrasts between Moses and Jesus, and we know from Philo's writings that the place of Moses in Jewish faith was a key issue in Alexandria. The theology of Alexandrian congregations was heavily influenced by the Hellenist movement that brought the gospel to Egypt.

Even more remarkable are the ties between Egypt, the Hellenist theology, and the Gospel of John. The "Hymn to the Logos" that opens the Gospel (Jn 1:1–18) so resembles elements of Philo's writings that the similarities cannot be accidental. This Gospel also is the one that speaks most fully of the body of the risen Christ replacing the temple at Jerusalem as the center of valid worship. It replaces the law of Judaism with Jesus' profound command, *"Love one another as I have loved you."* In the Hellenists' ministry, we may have discovered both the source of the Christian Church in Egypt and some of the raw material that went into the Gospel of John.

The tie between the Egyptian Church and the Hellenist movement is given additional credence when the ministry of Apollos is added to the mix. Described in Acts (18:23–25) as *"a Jew, a native of Alexandria, an eloquent man, well versed in the scriptures, instructed in the way of the Lord; and fervent in spirit,"* Apollos represented the best that the Hellenist movement had to offer. Reaching deeply into the Hellenist Jewish community already resident in Alexandria, the Hellenist Christian communities instructed their people in the Scriptures, produced persons of fervent spirit, and nurtured their people in the ways of Jesus the Christ.

Another remarkable thing was about to occur. The Hellenist gospel did not remain in Alexandria but moved on to Ephesus. Apollos, we are told, acting upon the missionary tradition of the Hellenist movement, went from Alexandria to Ephesus (18:24). His presence there is our first evidence that the Hellenist movement was to have fundamental influence not only in the great Christian centers of Antioch and Alexandria but in the equally important center of Ephesus.

An additional influence of the Hellenist movement on the congregation in Ephesus was soon to come in the person of Philip. Philip, whom we left talking on the Gaza Road with the finance minister of the kingdom of Ethiopia, had gone north along the coastal highway until he reached Caesarea. He stayed in Caesarea for at least twenty years, living with his four unmarried daughters who became notable in the region for their prophesying (Acts 21:8). Presumably, his being able to stay that long in this community meant that this congregation now began to take on characteristics of the Hellenist branch of the movement and may have become the leading Hellenist congregation in the Middle Eastern area.

Philip's time in Caesarea came to an abrupt end shortly before the Jewish Revolt in 66 C.E. Sensing the tensions that were soon to break out in open warfare between Jewish zealots and Roman legionnaires and wanting to escape from the dangers to come, Philip, with other members of the Caesarean congregation, migrated to Ephesus. His tomb, and that of his daughters, will be pointed out to anyone visiting this city today.

Here then is the vast irony of the Christian Hellenist movement. Disputatious from the beginning, it caused such a rift in the Jesus movement that it split the group in two. Yet, God used this breach in the Disciples' unity to carry out ministry in Samaria, Caesarea, Antioch, Alexandria and Ephesus, to name only a few of its centers of influence, where it might never have gone had this catastrophe not occurred.

vi

Based on the above, a summary of the beliefs and actions of the Hellenists within the Greek-speaking synagogues is possible. As seen in Table 4, an interconnected series of beliefs and actions contributed to a split by the Hellenists from certain Jewish traditions. A quick scan of Table 4 shows distinct contrasts with both the Disciples and the Brethren. Something was different on almost all the thirteen major points of comparison.

The differences are so apparent that it is impossible to identify which specific ones precipitated a split, including differences in the languages that predominated in the synagogues, Greek in the Hellenist synagogues versus Hebrew in the synagogues and congregations of the Disciples and Brethren. Differences in the cultural backgrounds of Hellenists in interacting with non-Jewish or non-Christian Hellenists also contributed to differences in their interpretations of theologies and ethics. Torah-observant Jews tried to separate themselves from other ethnic groups of the Roman Empire. Hellenist Jews sought contact with their gentile and pagan neighbors. Torah-observant Jews, as well as Torah-observant Brethren, followed the ethic set out in Leviticus 19:18, "Love your neighbor as yourself." The Hellenists emended that to Jesus saying to them, "Love one another as I have loved you." (Jn 13:14)

The "love one another" ethic focuses on fellowship, most obviously within and among congregants but also, according to Jesus' parable, love of even reviled "neighbors" (Samaritans, Jn 4:9; Lk 10:29–37) in the widest possible sense. The Hellenists' focus was on each other in collective fellowship with one another, and in embracing such fellowship in a variety of settings. This difference is highly emphasized in the formulations of ethics in the gospel of John compared to those of Mark and Matthew.

The reason for this has to do with the fact that the Hellenists were starting from a different position, based on the theology of Jesus being God incarnate and Son of Humankind. This theological stance is built on that of the Disciples, but it interprets Jesus as Messiah to Israel as originally constituted, as a people chosen to serve *all* peoples and not Jews alone. Since Hellenists were more likely than the other parties to represent a dominant culture in the world at this time, they could easily see their roles as based on this theological tradition which would have led them to the outcome that Jesus was the incarnate God, bringing this good news to all people who are open to hearing it. From this perspective Jesus' implicit teachings on theology are consistent with his ethics of loving one another, where the "others" are interpreted in the broadest possible sense, as all people.

Table 4. Summary of Actions and Beliefs Among the Hellenists Compared to the Twelve Disciples and the Brethren.

Parties	The Twelve Disciples	Brethren	Hellenists	Apostles
Beginning Event	Jesus's call in Galilee	Coming of the Spirit at Pentecost	Split with Hebrew speakers and their practices	
Governance	Cephas; The Twelve, the Assembly of 70	James; Elders	Seven Deacons; Philip; Beloved Disciple	
Mission Targets	Synagogues in Galilee, Gaza	Hebrew-speaking synagogues	Greek-speaking synagogues	
Composition of Party	Jewish men in leadership, some women	Jewish men and their families	Greek-speaking Jews, men and women	
Places of Worship	Temple, synagogues, house churches	Temple, synagogues, house churches	Synagogues, house churches	
Circumcision	Jewish men and proselytes before the Jerusalem Conference; only Jewish men after	Jewish men	Jewish men	
Food Laws	Kept, then did not	Kept all kosher laws	Did or did not keep laws	
Marriage Laws	Married Jewish women	Married Jewish women	Married Jewish women	

Parties	The Twelve Disciples	Brethren	Hellenists	Apostles
Theological Self-Understanding	Successor to Israel	Covenant renewed	New Israel or "Israel as originally constituted"	
Role of Jesus	Servant of God	Designated as Messiah at death, Son of David	Son of Humankind, Incarnate of God	
Primary Ethical Principle	"Take up cross, follow me"	"Seek God's righteousness"	"Love one another as I have loved you"	
Writings	Mark 1st Peter	Matthew James Jude Revelation	John Hebrews Letters of John	
Terminating Event	Death of leaders under Herod Agrippa	Death of James & leaders, Jewish war 66–79 C.E.	Continued after 70 C.E.	

Because the Hellenists were "representative" of a dominant culture in the Roman world, they were relatively eclectic in their adherence to Jewish traditions. Some of them kept the food, circumcision, and marriage laws while others did not. Some met in "house" congregations; others only in synagogues. Apparently, most had seven "deacons" in their congregational governance to care for the necessities of life among the entire congregation, but others followed the Hebrew tradition of male-only "elders" to run their affairs. The governing bodies included in their fellowships former Jews, "god-fearing" proselytes to the Jewish faith, and both men and women. These acts set them apart from the Disciples and the Brethren.

Due to their ethics, their theology, their family practices, and their congregations' governance, they had widespread appeal to other Greek speakers of the dominant culture. Conversions to the Jesus movement were relatively widespread among both Jews and gentiles, and these successes permitted them to survive and continue their evangelizing ministries beyond the destruction of the temple in 70 C.E

CHAPTER 5

The Apostles

The leading figure in the Apostles movement was a man known as Paul of Tarsus. When we first see him in the Book of Acts, he was called Saul, a Hebrew name.

In some unnamed capacity other than to hold garments, Saul was present at the stoning of Stephen, and he was apparently in agreement with the action. He was soon delegated, proably by the Brethren of Jerusalem, to travel to Damascus to find anyone there who belonged to the Way (one of the names used by the Hellenists to describe their movement, since Jesus said, *"I am the Way."*), men and women, and to bring them bound to Jerusalem (Acts 9:2). In his Letter to the Galatians (1:13–14), Paul described his attitude at that time: *"I persecuted the church of God violently and tried to destroy it; and I advanced in Judaism beyond many of my own age among my people, so extremely zealous was I for the traditions of my fathers."* But Saul was soon to become Paul. Jesus the Christ appeared to him in a vision and set him on a new mission. Paul's conversion to Christian faith was an act of such great importance to the early church that it is described in four different ways in Acts and in Galatians.

The first account of Paul's transformation (Acts 9:1-26) seems to be the one that circulated among the Disciples, the first of the groups described above. Paul's mission to Damascus caused havoc *"among the disciples."* (9:1) As he approached Damascus, a light from heaven flashed around him. Paul fell to the ground and heard a voice saying to him, "Saul, Saul, why do you persecute me?" Paul asked, "Who are you." The voice said, "I am Jesus, whom you are persecuting." Paul was blinded by the light and the voice and needed to be led by the hand into Damascus.

To Paul's surprise a Disciple named Ananias befriended Saul and interpreted to him the meaning of his experiences (9:10-19). For several days Paul remained with the Disciples at Damascus (9:19b). It was Disciples who lowered him over the wall to safety (9:25), and it was to the Disciples in Jerusalem that he first reported when he returned to the Holy City (9:26). "Disciples" play the main roles in this account.

The second account (22:2–21) appears to have been written from the point of view of the Brethren. Acts says that Paul addressed his hearers in the Hebrew language (22:2), and in this report he emphasized his Jewish background and education (22:3). Ananias was called not a Disciple but a *"devout man according to the law, well spoken of by all the Jews"* (22:12). In this account, the risen lord appeared twice to Paul, once on the road to Damascus, but the second time *"while (he) was praying in the temple"* (22:7). All these are themes beloved by the Brethren.

The third account (26:1–23) seems to be the official account of the Apostles themselves of Paul's conversion. In this account there is no Ananias to interpret the event for Paul, no dramatic escape from Damascus. There is a job description given to Paul that sounds like his Apostolic calling: *"I have appeared to you,"* said the Christ, *"to appoint you to serve and bear witness to the things in which you have seen me and to those in which I will appear to you, delivering you from the people and from the Gentiles—to whom I send you to open their eyes, that they may turn from darkness to light and from the power of Satan to God, that they may receive forgiveness of sins and a place among those who are sanctified by faith in me"* (26:16–18).

Paul's own account of the appearance of the risen Christ to him (Gal 1:11–17; 2:20; 3:1–14) intrigues us most. Paul tells of a transcendent breakthrough into his life that changed him totally.

A passage in Galatians 3:1–14 sets out the struggle Paul was having within himself over accepting the Christian faith. This internal conflict had two facets to it, and each needed to be resolved before Paul could become a follower of the risen Christ.

One facet was the conflict between "Christ" and "law." The law said to Paul, *"Cursed be everyone who does not abide by all things written in the law to do them"* (3:10). Paul knew that Christ had not done *"everything written in the law,"* and he knew that he personally could not claim to have done so, either (Rom 7:13–24).

Did Jesus' seemingly offhand attitude toward the law nullify his ministry? Did Paul's own impotence in the face of the law's commands render void and futile his own life? No, said Paul, for as he read further in the law he came upon this statement: *"Cursed be everyone who hangs upon a tree!"* (Gal 3:13). Twice cursed was Jesus, once for not keeping all the law and a second time for hanging on a tree. But, said Paul, the latter curse cancelled out the former. By hanging on the tree, Christ had wiped away his own cavalier behavior toward the law; He also wiped away the impotence Paul had felt at not being able to keep it. Now Christ, and all who were Christ's, were freed from the clutching tentacles of the law and could live a new life based on Christ's spirit. Paul's method of reasoning was an exercise in rabbinic exegesis, perhaps unconvincing to us today, but it convinced Paul. From the moment he had resolved his own question, he was able to say, *"Christ redeemed us from the curse of the law, having become a curse for us"* (3:13a).

The second issue Paul confronted concerned the relationship of Jews and gentiles in the Christian faith. Paul had to solve this problem before he could honestly preach Christ to the gentiles.

The problem centered on the promise of God given to Abraham in Genesis 12:1–3. God had promised Abraham that

God would make of him a great nation and that by Abraham all the families of the earth shall bless themselves. On the basis of this passage, the Jews claimed that the promise was given exclusively to them. It was given to Abraham, and they were the sons of Abraham and the inheritors of this promise.

But did that Old Testament statement exclude gentiles from the promise? No, said Paul, reflecting on Scripture. Abraham received the promise not because he was a Jew but because he was a person of faith. It is not Jews only but *"all persons of faith (who) are blessed by the faithful Abraham"* (Gal 3:6-9)... *In Jesus Christ the blessing of Abraham might come upon the gentiles, that we might receive the promise of the spirit through faith"* (3:14).

As Paul was working through these problems of mind and heart, the Transcendent One in the person of the risen Christ broke into his life. The Greek word *apocaluptein* was used by Paul to describe his experience. The primary meaning of *apocaluptein* is "to lay open what has been veiled or covered up." A nuance of this is that the *apocaluptein* comes in a sudden or even a violent way. Paul's *apocaluptein* carried both meanings. In this moment Paul's past, his present, and his future took on new meaning in terms of Jesus Christ.

Paul's future was to be that of preaching Christ among the gentiles (Gal 1:16). Paul as Saul had been zealous for Judaism. He had been born into a Jewish family, he had come from the Hebrew and not the Hellenist side of diaspora Judaism, he had studied at the feet of Judaism's greatest teachers. In the name of the Jewish faith (or perhaps in the name of the Torah-observant synagogues), he had persecuted the Jesus movement congregations. After the breakthrough, that part of his life was over for Paul. His mission was to preach Christ among the gentiles, and he would channel all his talent and energy into doing this.

Accepting this new mission for Christ put his past life into perspective. Why had he been born and reared a Hebrew in an Hellenistic city like Tarsus? Why did he speak and write both Hebrew and Greek? Of what use was his Roman citizenship? Why had he been given such physical energy, natural intellect, and spiritual talents that he was able to *"advance in Judaism beyond many of my own age among my people"* (1:14)? For what purpose was he at the moment free from family obligations? What would he do with the bubbling physical energy he possessed?

In the moment of Christ's breakthrough, Paul's past came together for him. God had provided him with precisely these talents and abilities so that he could do the work that God had long ago destined for him. As God had called Jeremiah to be a prophet, so God called Paul to be an apostle. *"God set me apart from the womb and called me by divine grace, so that I might preach Christ to the gentiles"* (Gal 1:15–16).

What this revelation of Christ meant for his life in the present, Paul was to set out in 2:19–20: *"I have been crucified with Christ. No longer I live, but lives in me Christ. And the life I now live in flesh I live by faith in the son of God who loved me and gave himself for me."* Paul was overwhelmed with the Christ within him. *En emoi,* the Greek phrase for his internalization of Christ, appears both in Galatians 1:16, where Paul described Christ's breakthrough into his life, and in 2:20, where he described what the breakthrough meant to him. It meant that Christ had taken full possession of Paul. As the Heidelberg Catechism (Question 76) was later to say in describing the experience of the real presence of Christ in the Lord's Supper, "Christ has become bone of my bone, flesh of my flesh, will of my will, thought of my thought, word of my word, action of my action, life of my life."

From the moment of Christ's apocalyptic coming to him, Paul was dead to all the things of the world, both its miseries and its glories, and alive only to Christ. *"Far be it from me,"* he wrote to the Galatian Christians at the end of his letter to them (6:14), *"to glory (in anything) except in the cross of our Lord Jesus Christ, by which the world is crucified unto me and I unto the world."*

ii

The first time we see the Apostles together as a group, they were already experimenting with what it meant to be followers of Jesus Christ. Luke recorded the event near the beginning of the Acts (2:43–47):

And fear came upon every soul and many wonders and signs were done through the apostles. And all who believed were together and had all things in common: and they sold their possessions and goods and distributed them to all, as any had need. And day by day, attending the temple together and breaking bread in their homes, they partook of food with glad and generous hearts, praising God and having favor with all the people. And the Lord added to their number day by day those who were being saved.

The locale of the report was Jerusalem, for they were near enough to the temple to go to it daily for worship. The report is undated, but it must have taken place in the early days of the first fine careless rapture in the early Jesus movement, for the Apostles were already engaged in the kind of social experimentation that was to distinguish the group from the other parties in the early church. A listing of the distinctive characteristics they were already rehearsing gives some idea of the venturesome spirit the Apostles were adopting.

1. They worshipped daily in the Temple. This related them to the Disciples and the Brethren but not to the Hellenists. In these earliest days they considered themselves to be fully Jewish in this deepest expression of the faith–worshipping God in God's temple.
2. They met in homes of members in order to break bread together. This act probably meant that they were celebrating the meal over which the Lord had presided on the night in which he was betrayed (Cor 11:23–24),

and they believed that the Lord was present with them in spirit when they ate and drank together. To the worship in the temple they had added the kind of intimate and communal worship that Jesus had observed in the days of his visible ministry,

3. They engaged in trying to produce signs and wonders in the name of Jesus as Christ. When their attempts at healings and exorcisms succeeded, they felt that truly the spirit of Christ was working through them.

4. They put the resurrection of Jesus Christ at the center of their ministry (Acts 4:33). Unlike the Disciples, whose leaders had been with Jesus from the time of his baptism by John until he was taken up on the cross and then ascended into the heavens, the Apostles had not known Jesus in his earthly days. They knew him only through the resurrection visions that had been afforded them and the reports about him by other groups of the faithful. Their testimony was not so much to his life and ministry as it was to the grace and peace that had come to them through his resurrection.

5. From the beginning this group was made up of both women and men. We shall speak of this later, but it is important to note at this point.

6. The most strikingly distinctive feature of their fellowship was their attempt to hold all things in common. Acts (4:34–36) relates that they sold even their lands and their houses and deposited the proceeds with the Apostles.

This is the way in which we meet Barnabas, the first member of the group introduced to us by name; he sold a field which belonged to him and laid the money from the sale at the Apostles' feet. The Apostles then would distribute the money to anyone of their group who had need.

Not many religious groups of that day did this as rigorously as the Apostles were attempting to do it. Judaism was not then or later a faith that exhibited the kind of monastic inclinations that this practice would result in. Other Jewish groups, like the members of the various synagogues, recognized their responsibility to care for people in need, their widows and children and orphans and the like, but the money they gathered to do this came from collections in the synagogue and not from sale of their dwelling places. The few groups in Judea which were monastic, like the Qumran fellowship on the shores of the Dead Sea, had quickly learned that they had to withdraw from society in order to set up a utopian community like this. Could it be done in the way the Apostles were attempting? A huge question-mark hung over the venture.

This endeavor soon brought disaster to one of their families and, by extension, to the group itself. Ananias sold a piece of property. With his wife's connivance, he withheld from the Apostles some of the money from the sale. What they most likely kept for themselves was the wife's *ketuba,* the amount of money her husband would have had to pay her if he divorced her unilaterally or which his heirs would pay her if he died before she did. We can be deeply sympathetic with the couple's reasoning. It is fine to rely on God fully, husband and wife said to one another, but perhaps we should retain this much for ourselves in case the community's present system for taking care of widows' needs runs out of steam, as well it may do sooner or later. Ananias and Sapphira agreed with one another on this matter, and they withheld for themselves a portion of the sale money when they brought it to the Apostles.

The Apostles came down hard on them. "You did not have to make this contribution to God," they said, "but voluntarily you made a vow to God that you would donate this money for this use. Why did you lie to the Holy Spirit and to God?"

Ananias was struck so deeply by this curse that he fell down and died. Jews knew of situations that were punished by death at the hands of heaven, and this sudden death could have resulted from heart failure caused by the emotional stress the man was under. Three hours later, his wife was put under similar stress. Not knowing what had happened to her husband, she was confronted by the Apostles. *"Did you sell the land for so much?"* they asked. When she said they did, they accosted her as they had previously accosted her husband, and the result was the same. In fear and trembling, she died, and the same burial detail that had put her husband into the ground laid her beside him.

It was not a moment of which the Apostles were proud, and we can see it in the next line of the report: *"Great fear came upon the whole church, and upon all who heard of these things"* (5:11). Apparently, the deaths of Ananias and Sapphira caused vast soul-searching among the leadership of the Apostles, for they abandoned the practice at once. Never again in the Acts are we told that this group, or any group in the early Christian movement, tried to develop a fellowship where all things were held in common, to each according to their need and from each according to their ability to pay.

iii

The beginnings of the group called "Apostles" are hidden from view. They seem to have been Jews, both Hebrews and Hellenists (that is, Aramaic-speaking and Greek-speaking), whose homes were outside Jerusalem. Barnabas was from Cyprus, Paul was from Tarsus, Junia and Andronicus were from Ephesus or Rome. "Place of residence" may have been one clear matter that distinguished the Apostles from the Hellenists described previously. The Hellenists of Acts 6–8 were native to Judea and Galilee, precincts where Jesus had ministered, while the Apostles were people who had come to the Holy City from outside this region.

The Hellenists and Apostles did not get along well with each other. Saul was described as holding coats when Stephen was killed, and when Saul tried to get in contact with the group in Jerusalem, he was rebuffed. When the Disciples underwent a fierce persecution following the death of Stephen, the Apostles were specifically excluded from that: *"...great persecution arose against the church in Jerusalem,"* said Luke (Acts 8:2–3), *"and all were scattered... except the apostles."* Whatever the cause of their immunity—it may have been that they were willing to worship in the temple, whereas the Hellenists were less willing—the enmity between the two groups was great and only seemed to be healed when Apollos came to Ephesus and then went on to Corinth where Paul was ministering.

The meaning of the title "Apostle" is obscure. The word appeared only rarely in Greek literature before it was used in the Jesus movement. Originally it had to do with seafaring, and it indicated the dispatch of a fleet, the fleet itself, a naval expedition, the admiral of the expedition, then a passport and a bill of lading. Rabbinic Judaism adopted its usage from the Christians to describe the work of a commissioned agent who was to act in the name of another. This agent might contract an engagement of marriage, manage a divorce proceeding, slaughter the Passover lamb, or even represent the Jewish authorities to the Jews of the diaspora.

Christian usage of the word tended to fall in the middle of these two clusters of meaning. "Apostles" often had to do with the sea. They went on long journeys to carry out the work of Christ. In transacting this work, they acted in a representative capacity. They were, as a direct translation of the word implies, the "Sent Ones" whom, they felt, Christ had commissioned to go into the world as his special agents.

The roster of the "Sent Ones" is extensive. All these persons were included in it:

Paul and Barnabas
Junia and Andronicus (Rom 16:7)
Barnabas and Mark
Aquila and Priscilla (Acts 18:28)
Gaius and Aristarchus (Acts 19:29)
Zenas and Apollos (Titus 3:13)

Tychicus and Onesimus (Col 4:7)
Aristarcus and Secundus
Gaius and Timothy
Titus and an unnamed brother ((2 Cor 12:18)
Tychicus and Trophemus (Acts 20:4)

Travelling in pairs to such diverse places as Corinth and
Ephesus, Crete and Syria, Colossae, Jerusalem and Rome,
they roamed the world between Italy and Judea.

iv

If we know little of the origins of the Apostles and not
much more about the exact meaning of their name, we do
know of the work that they did.

They founded congregations wherever they went, and
they worked with churches already in existence when they
came to a community to which the Jesus movement had already come. Operating on the theory that these men and
women who had come from areas outside Judea and Galilee
could minister more adequately to similar areas than could
persons who were strangers to them, the Apostles became
the "Sent Ones" to areas in which the Jesus movement was
struggling or was presently nonexistent.

First, Barnabas was sent to Antioch to work with the
church that had already been established there. He was successful in adding many souls to it. He went beyond Antioch
to Tarsus to look for Saul, and the two returned together to
Antioch where they labored for a year (Acts 11:19–26). Their
period of service to that church ended when they brought a
relief offering from the Antioch church to the Brethren and
elders in Jerusalem.

Next (13:1–9) they were sent to Cilicia, near Paul's home
area of Tarsus, and to Cyprus, which was the home island of
Barnabas. In Salamis and Paphos on Cyprus, they went to
the synagogues to preach the Christian message. Crossing
to the mainland west of Tarsus, they worked for a period in

Galatia. Luke at this point inserted a sample of their missionary methodology and their message.

> *On the Sabbath day they went into the synagogue and sat
> down. After the reading of the law and the prophets, the
> rulers of the synagogue sent to them, saying, "Brethren,
> if you have any word of exhortation for the people, say
> it." So Paul stood up, and motioning with his hand said...
> (13:13–16).*

It was a regular service of worship in the synagogue to which
they had gone, and their "word of exhortation" was presented in response to what was read in the Scriptures. The
freedom of the synagogue to listen to many points of view
permitted the Apostles to speak, and they were invited to do
so by those in charge of the community and its worship. The
message they presented emphasized the following:

1. It was addressed to both Jews and Gentiles. "*Men of Is-
    rael,*" Paul said, "*and you who fear God*" (13:16). These
    were not synonymous. The "men of Israel" were the
    Jewish men who belonged to the synagogue. "You who
    fear God" referred to the gentile godfearers who were
    attached to this particular synagogue. That Paul ad-
    dressed his message to both groups is seen again when
    he came to the major point of his sermon: "*Brethren,
    sons of the family of Abraham, and those among you who
    fear God*" (13:26).
2. While he addressed both groups, Paul did not forget
    the priority in faith held by the Jews. Speaking to those
    Jews who had made a favorable response to his mes-
    sage but who had come under attack by their fellow
    believers, Paul said, "*It was necessary that the word of
    God should be spoken first to you*" (13:46). This was the
    practice of the Apostles. Their first address was to the
    Jews. As Paul was to say later in his letter to the church
    at Rome, "*To the Jews belonged the law, the covenant,*

the Scriptures, Abraham and Moses and David, and from them Jesus Christ was born." (9:4ff)

It was only when the Jews did not respond to their message that the Apostles turned their attention to the gentiles, as Paul quickly said in this speech to the Galatian synagogue. *"But when you thrust the word of God from you and judge yourselves unworthy of eternal life, behold, we turn to the Gentiles"* (13:46b). When the Jews refused to hear their word, and by doing so had brought the judgment of God upon themselves, the Apostles' response was emphatic. Obeying the explicit command of Jesus, *"they shook off the dust from their feet against them"*—an act of great contempt in the eyes of mideastern people—*"and went on (to another town)"* (13:51).

3. The message they brought was one of salvation, and it came through the crucified and risen Christ. Jesus they described as the son of David, whom God said *"was a man after my own heart, who will do my will"* (13:22). From this man's lineage and in the spirit of his humble walk with God, God had brought to Israel a savior, Jesus, as God has promised. This Jesus was crucified when *"those who live in Jerusalem and their rulers asked Pilate to have him killed."* But unlike David, who was laid beside his fathers and experienced the corruption of the grave, Jesus was saved from this corruption by God *"as God raised him from the dead. For many days Jesus appeared to those who came up with him from Galilee to Jerusalem, who now became his witnesses to the people"* (13:30–31).

4. What was the purpose behind Jesus' crucifixion and resurrection? *"Through this man,"* said Paul, *"forgiveness of sins is proclaimed to you"* (13:38). The forgiveness offered by Paul and Barnabas to the people of the synagogues of Galatia differed in important respects from the forgiveness Peter had preached to the people of Jerusalem.

Peter had said that the forgiveness of Christ covered the sins of the Jews who had cried out for Jesus to be crucified. If anyone now living in Jerusalem should repent of the sins of their fellow members of the synagogues, God through Christ would forgive their sins and would accept them into the new community of Christ. In Galatia, Paul said that anyone who believes in Christ is *"freed from everything from which you could not be freed by the law of Moses"* (13:3). The requirements of the law of Moses–to be part of the covenant people one needed to be circumcised, sacrifice in the temple, keep the food laws of the Jewish people–did not offer freedom but slavery. Once a person bought into those practices, this person was enslaved to them forever. But once Christ bought the person and the person bought into Christ, this person was freed from those false requirements which did not bring life, and he or she was ushered into the new life. Paul twice described this new life as "eternal life" (13:46,48), life like that lived by God in the eternity of God's fellowship opened through Jesus Christ.

Such was the basic message of the group called Apostles. The Letter to the Galatians was probably written at the end of this first ministry of Paul and Barnabas in the Galatian cities of Derbe, Lystra, and Iconium, just before Paul went to Jerusalem for the important council to which he was summoned (Acts 15). If this is so, "Galatians" becomes the first of Paul's letters and contains the earliest record we have of the faith of the apostolic community.

v

Galatians contains other startling statements. Two stand out for special attention.

1. In Galatians, Paul quoted the charter for participation in the congregations of the Apostles. *"... for in Christ Jesus*

you are all children of God through faith. For, as many of you as were baptized into Christ have clothed yourselves with Christ. There is no longer Jew nor Greek, there is no longer slave nor free, there is no longer male and female. For you are all one in Christ" (Gal 3:26–28). No more inclusive charter than this has ever been written for Christian churches.

No longer Jew nor Greek: Persons of both religions and cultures were welcomed fully into the fellowship of the Apostles, and no distinction was drawn between them in sharing in the benefits of Christ.

No longer slave nor free: Class distinctions also were abolished in the Apostles' congregations. The slave could sit at the same table of the Lord as could his or her owner. While those outside the fellowship might be horrified at this example of egalitarianism, no one within was to raise any questions about its propriety.

No longer male and female: The original charter in Greek has "male" and "female" connected by the conjunction "and." By doing so, it was referring the participant to God's original intent of creation as recorded in Genesis: "So God created humanity in God's own image, in the image of God God created us; male and female God created us" (1:27). God made male and female, together, to be one humanity, each with the same rights and privileges and not to be separated as the Torah-observant Jew separated them. In their churches the Apostles were seeing that God's original intent was being recreated.

We need hardly illustrate the many ways this charter was woven into the fabric of the apostolic fellowship. Jews like Barnabas had leadership in the Apostles' congregations and Greeks like Titus did. Free Roman citizens like Paul sat down at the table of their fellowships, and so did slaves like Onesimus. Women and men like Priscilla and Aquila and Junia and Andronicus together preached and taught the gospel. Men received the gospel from women and women from men. Baptism was at the heart of this. While circumcision was not open to women (and thus had excluded women from the inner circle of Jewish life for more than five centuries, from the time when circumcision was formally declared to be at the center of God's covenant with the people), baptism was open to all. Anyone who was baptized, male and female, Jew or Greek, slave or free, had put on Christ. In two thousand years of striving, the church has never fully caught up with the charter set by the Apostles within the first two decades of life in the Apostles' congregations.

2. Equally startling is Paul's list toward the end of his letter of the *"fruit of the spirit"* (Gal 5:22). Nine special graces are mentioned as deriving from the spirit of Jesus Christ and as being the special possession of the Christian community. What is not obvious in the translation of these words, but what is clear in the original manuscripts, is that three of the words represent the special longings of Jewish people, three are the qualities of life sought among the Jews in the synagogues of the Hellenistic world, and three refer to the special virtues of Greek life that Greek teachers tried to instil in their students.

"Love, joy, peace" are the special Jewish words; *"patience, kindness, and goodness"* are the Hellenistic words; *"faithfulness, gentleness, and self-control"* are the Greek graces prized above all others. Paul says that all these are given to us through the spirit of Christ; all these are found together only in the life of Christ. The "fruit of the spirit" draws together the total makeup of the apostolic communities. Jewish people are there, and proselytes from the communities of the Hellenistic synagogues, and godfearers who had not yet united fully with the Jewish faith but are welcomed into the fellowship of the Christians. All these find in Christ the longed-for fulfilment of their lives.

Surrounding "the fruit of the spirit" are those ethical principles by which Paul lived and which he recommended to his congregations. The first indicated that Paul had already learned of Jesus' great commandments: *"...you were called to freedom, brethren; only do not use your freedom as an opportunity for the flesh, but through love be servants of one another. For the whole law is fulfilled in one word, 'You shall love your neighbor as yourself'"* (5:13–14). Paul restated "the law of Christ" into a supplemental principle, *"Bear one another's burdens, and so fulfill the law of Christ"* (6:2). His ethical thinking was deeply related to the fact of Jesus' crucifixion, but it was also built on that of Peter, the Brethren, and even the Hellenists. *"Those who belong to Christ Jesus have crucified the flesh with its passions and desires. If we live by the Spirit, let us also walk by the Spirit"* (5:24–25). He described some of the actions required to "walk by the spirit." *"Let us have no self-conceit, no provoking of one another, no envy of one another"* (5:26). Underscoring what he had just said, he wrote out in his own handwriting so all could see, *"Neither circumcision counts for anything, nor uncircumcision, but a new creation"* (6:15), the person and the community transformed into something totally new by the spirit of Jesus Christ.

vi

The arduous journeys of faith by Paul and Barnabas, representatives of the "Sent Ones," are documented throughout the Book of Acts. The journeys took them from Galatia to Antioch. There Paul was confronted with what he considered the apostasy of both Cephas and Barnabas in withdrawing, at the insistence of James, from eating with the gentiles of the Christian community, thereby voiding the apostolic charter. From there they went to Jerusalem for the council in which the issue was adjudicated. Paul with Silas, one of the group of the Brethren, then transmitted the agreement arrived at in the conference to his congregations in Galatia, Syria, and Cilicia, while Barnabas and Mark returned with it to Cyprus. Going beyond Cilicia, Paul wanted to turn north to Bithynia and the Black Sea to carry on his work, but the spirit of Christ would not permit this, so he crossed instead to Macedonia.

At Philippi, Paul founded a new congregation. At Thessalonika and Berea he did the same, each time presenting himself in the synagogues as a means of gaining entrance for his message. At Athens, he found no synagogue. He could only preach on a high rock atop the agora near the acropolis. His sermon attracted attention but developed no commitment. At Corinth, he either founded a congregation or worked with one already there. He stayed at Corinth for nearly two years. Having gathered his share of the collection for the "Poor of Jerusalem" as he had agreed to do many years before, he retraced his steps and headed for Jerusalem, pausing for nearly two and a half years in Ephesus and working with congregations there. Back to Caesarea he came, again to Ephesus, Troas, Assos, Mitylene, Samos, Miletus, Cos, Rhodes, Patera, Syria, Tyre, Caesarea again, Jerusalem again. Even today we marvel at the stamina that took Paul to these places. Then came his journey in irons to Rome, his final imprisonment, and his death.

The work of other Apostles was not traced in Acts, but we can be assured they too were carrying the message of Jesus Christ wherever they could. Founding congregations, working with congregations, providing hospitality for those visiting from other places, performing pastoral duties, trying to adjudicate matters of dispute within the congregations, dealing with ethical questions, participating in worship—these activities and more are spoken of in the lengthy literature that came from Paul's hand and from the hand of those who shared his work.

vii

Nearly half the writings in the New Testament come from the community of the Apostles—the letter to the Romans, the correspondence Paul directed to Corinth and to Philippi, the letters to the Galatians and Thessalonians, the personal note to Philemon. Other letters emanated from the Apostolic communities, among them the general letter called "Ephesians," its companion piece Colossians, the letters to Timothy and Titus, the second letter to the Thessalonians. Even the epic work called Luke-Acts seems to be related to the apostolic community. Those who wish can explore the spirit of the Apostolic communities by acquainting themselves with these documents.

Unlike some of the other communities of the early church which we have modeled, the community of the Apostles did not disappear. Paul died, along with Barnabas and the other original members of the fellowship, but their communities were commuted into other forms of church life designed to meet the new challenges of the day. The spirit of the Apostles continued to break through into the world. Martin Luther and Martin Luther King come to mind as two who were captured by it, and Karl Barth brought a whole new spirit into church life in the 20th century when he read Paul's Letter to the Romans. The ideals they erected of the inclusive church opened by baptism into Jesus Christ beckons us still today.

viii

The Apostles generated a different set of beliefs and actions on the thirteen major issues in the summaries we have presented. They discovered early in their work that some gentiles as well as some Jews responded positively to what they believed about Jesus as Christ. Thus gentiles became a major "target audience," even if the Apostles also worked with both Hebrew-speaking and Greek-speaking Jews.

Theirs was a message of inclusiveness. Under the ethical tenet of sharing one another's burdens, it was logical for them to understand God as the God of all people with, potentially, none being excluded—rather than of just one ethnic group. Jews, Greeks, men, women, slave and free were all welcomed into their fellowship. The same ethical ideal

Table 5. Summary of the Apostles' Actions and Beliefs on Thirteen Major Issues.

Parties	The Twelve Disciples	Brethren	Hellenists	Apostles
Beginning Event	Jesus's call in Galilee	Coming of the Spirit at Pentecost	Split with Hebrew speakers and their practices	Recognized possibilities for extending the movement through missions to Gentiles
Governance	Cephas; The Twelve, the Assembly of 70	James; Elders	Seven Deacons; Philip; Beloved Disciple	Paul; Assembly of the Apostles, Barnabas
Mission Targets	Synagogues in Galilee, Gaza	Hebrew-speaking synagogues	Greek-speaking synagogues	Diaspora synagogues both Jew and Greek; God-fearers; Gentile friends
Composition of Party	Jewish men in leadership, some women	Jewish men and their families	Greek-speaking Jews, men and women	Jew, Greek; slave, free; women, men
Places of Worship	Temple, synagogues, house churches	Temple, synagogues, house churches	Synagogues, house churches	Temple, synagogues, house churches
Circumcision	Jewish men and proselytes before the Jerusalem Conference; only Jewish men after	Jewish men	Jewish men	Jewish men could be cicumcised, but Gentiles need not

Parties	The Twelve Disciples	Brethren	Hellenists	Apostles
Food Laws	Kept, then did not	Kept all kosher laws	Did or did not keep laws	Tried, but failed to keep provisions of the Conference
Marriage Laws	Married Jewish women	Married Jewish women	Married Jewish women	Marriage open to all
Theological Self-Understanding	Successor to Israel	Covenant renewed	New Israel or "Israel as originally constituted"	Those "in Christ"
Role of Jesus	Servant of God	Designated as Messiah at death, Son of David	Son of Humankind, Incarnate of God	Crucified and risen Christ
Primary Ethical Principle	"Take up cross, follow me"	"Seek God's righteousness"	"Love one another as I have loved you"	"Bear one another's burdens"
Writings	Mark 1st Peter	Matthew James Jude Revelation	John Hebrews Letters of John	Luke, Acts Romans Corinthians Galatians Ephesians Philppians Colossians Thessalonians Pastorals Philemon
Terminating Event	Death of leaders under Herod Agrippa	Death of James & leaders, Jewish war 66–70 C.E.	Continued after 70 C.E.	Continued after 70 C.E.

of inclusiveness was applied to the governance of the local congregations (*ecclesia*, in Greek). Everyone in the fellowship was eligible to participate in overall governance of their congregations' affairs. To them, even though Jesus had been crucified, and died, his resurrection was assured and God's Holy Spirit continued with them in their fellowships with one another.

Under the ethical principles of bearing one another's burdens and the equality among all persons which was its logical extension, the various laws of the Torah—circumcision, food laws, and marriage laws, which made Jews exclusive—were set aside. To set aside these rules made the party and its congregations more available to people from all walks of life. Such flexibility also made this party in the Jesus movement among the most vital. Consequently, this party's congregations continued to grow beyond 70 C.E. to eventually become dominant among the churches throughout the cities and villages of the Roman Empire, and, indeed, to continue even after the Roman Empire disappeared.

CHAPTER 6

The Jesus Movement in Practice

A Sociological Perspective

One of the important results accomplished in this study has been to bring flesh and blood to a theory that Adolph von Harnack set forth a century ago (Harnack, 1909). In his pioneering work, Harnack believed that he had found the source material used by Luke when Luke wrote the Acts of the Apostles. Harnack called them "Jerusalem Source A," "Jerusalem Source B," "Jerusalem-Caesarean Source," a "Pauline source," and an "Antiochene source." He assigned the source material used by Luke in chapters 2–15 in the following manner:

Jerusalem Source A	Jerusalem Source B	Jerusalem-Antiochene Source
3:15:16	2:1–47	6;1–8:4
8:5–40	5:17–42	12:25–15:35
9:31–11:18		
12:1–23		

He believed that chapters 16 through 28 consisted of an integrated source telling of the ministry of Paul (Harnack, pp. 188–189).

While our conclusions as to the source material in Acts displays a remarkable degree of similarity to Harnack's, we re-assigned the sources to the parties in the Jesus movement. We called Source A the work of the Twelve. Source B was the account of the Brothers. The Jerusalem-Antiochan source came from the Hellenists (the two cities were put together into one source because the Hellenists had missions in both Jerusalem and Antioch).

We made some suggested changes to his work. We assigned small portions of Acts chapters 2 and 4 to the Apostles. We also assigned 12:24–14:28 to the Apostles, since it is the first report of the Apostles' ministry. We assigned 15:1–35 to the Brethren, since it is the description of the Jerusalem conference, and it was told from their point of view. The "we" passages are from the Apostles. These were broken up by a lengthy passage, 21:17–24:27 that seems to come from the Brethren. It refers to elders, it names the Brethren very favorably in their relationships with Paul, and it quotes verbatim the decision made at Jerusalem. Paul never does that. We pick up the "we" passages at 25:1 and carry their story through almost to the end. Acts 28:23–31, the mundane ending of Paul's story, appears to be an addendum to the book, added by another hand; we suggest it is the Brethren's account of Paul's years in Rome.

Our look at Luke's use of sources results in the following:

TWELVE	BRETHREN	APOSTLES	HELLENISTS
1:1–26	2:1–41	2:42–47	
3:1–4:31		4:32–5:42	6:1–8:40
9:1–12:23	15:1–35	12:24–14:28	
		15:36–21:16	
	21:17–24:27	25:1–28:22	
	28:23–31		

To our minds these are not merely "sources." They are the accounts, coming first- or second-hand from four different parties, that Luke used to describe the work of each party of the Jesus movement. Regarding them as such brings us very close to the struggles of the parties we identified as they sought to present the good news (gospel) of Jesus Christ to the Roman world.

ii

A second important result of this study is theological as well as sociological. In our reading of the situation of the early Jesus movement, we find that, nearly from its beginning, within its first year at least, the Jesus movement consisted of four parties, not one. Four interpretations of the effect of Jesus on human society stand side by side in the pages of our New Testament. Four representations of his ministry are offered. Four sets of the meaning and mission of Jesus are explicated. Each party, working in its own environment, offered its own understanding of Jesus to the adherents of each group, to the participants of the other three groups, and to the world at large.

Attempts to overcome this fact of Christian life are numerous. Luke tried to bring the mission of the church into a single focus by his account of it. But he has not been able to hide the fact that he had source material from each of the four parties to deal with. Each group presented its own gospel as the chief one, but the judgment of the church in its first four centuries was that we needed four gospels, at least, and various letters and writings to set forth the true Christ to the world; when they established a canon of writings, all four gospels were contained in it. One church group or another, starting with the Brethren at a very early momemt in the life of the church, has tried to act as if it possesses the only truth of the faith and the only way that it can be practiced, just as some churches today maintain that their reading of the Scripture is the only possible one. To any who try to do one of the other of these things, we can only say, Beware! The Jesus movement has been pluralistic from its very beginning, and any attempt to deny this denies the fundamental history of the church's life and times.

iii

Jesus was certainly one of the most charismatic persons in history. His life deeply affected almost everyone he met—disciples, the seventy, people listening to the sermon on the mount, his family, even, according to the gospels, Pontius Pilate, the very man who oversaw his condemnation (Mt 27:24; Lk 23:4), and the centurion who oversaw the crucifixion (Mt 27:54; Lk 23:47). For one reason or another, Jesus' effect on people was very powerful. Was it due to his person?...his miracles?...his message?...to the people gathered about him? ...to the character of people most intimate with him?...to the love he showed them?

Certainly the ethical principles that Jesus espoused were unique in history up to his time. Repeatedly, Jesus promulgated a perspective on life that contrasted with the ethical principles both of the Roman Empire and of Jewish Law. He thoroughly eschewed violence and warfare as a way to peace. Even if the *pax Romana* was widely respected, its practice always set the Roman Emperor above everyone else, and Rome's legions assured, often quite ruthlessly, that people respected him. Meanwhile, Jesus maintained, *"Give unto Caesar that which is Caesar's, and unto God that which is God's"* (Mt 22:21, Mk 12:17, Lk 20:25). To Jesus, there was a huge difference between what he believed and the beliefs of Rome and Jerusalem.

Further, he asserted, *"The Kingdom of God is at hand"* (Mt 3:2, 4:17; Mk 1:15; Lk 10:9)—not in temporal powers yet to come, but in the present power of God and in the manner that people treat one another—*"Love one another as I have loved you"* (Jn 13:34); *"Bear one another's burdens"* (Gal 6:2); *"If a man forces you to go one mile, go two miles"* (Mt 5:41); *"Take up your cross and follow me"* (Mt 16:24; Mk 8:34, Mk 10:31; Lk 9:23); *"Seek first the Kingdom of God and his righ-*

teousness" (in "doing the right thing" to further God's Kingdom), and *"all these things will be yours as well"* (Mt 6:33, Lk
12:31).

Although these seem, as Reinhold Niebuhr wrote, "impossible ethical ideals," these ideals represented God's way, Jesus claimed, and can easily be seen as relevant to people's
lives. Moreover, when people have similar experiences in
their lives, they are in awe of them. But once Jesus provided
a conscious and understandable explanation of such experiences, they became experiences that people seek to have
repeatedly and not merely occasionally.

Such love-based experiences also stood out in gargantuan
terms compared to other possible alternatives in life under
the Roman Empire or under Jewish Law. Things routinely
sought in life pale by comparison. Power without love is ultimately not satisfying, and similarly for wealth without love,
community social status without love, obedience without
love; even devotion without love is unsatisfying (I Cor 13).

Jesus' primary ethical message of "love one another" as
a way of life, then, was compelling to people in providing
alternatives to life not otherwise found in "the world." This
was not a message of retreat to a "community of true be-
lievers" as in Qumran. This was certainly not a call to sur-
reptitious preparation for armed rebellion as with the Zealots. This was not a call for complete devotion in following
Torah Law, as with the Pharisees, or being collaborators
with the Roman Empire as with the Sadducees and the Sanhedrin. This was not a message to be stoically content with
one's place in life, as with the Stoics, or with "moderation
in all things" as Greek teachers and philosophers taught,
or to indulge oneself in pleasure-seeking through food and
drink as with most hedonists.

It was a message, as H. Richard Niebuhr, Daniel Day Williams, and James Gustafson described it in *The Purpose of the
Church and Its Ministry,* whereby people could legitimately,
without guilt or shame, share in joy in the presence of others, in gratitude for their gifts of their being with you and

one another, in respect for the "otherness" of others, and in loyalty to things to which they were mutually loyal among one another. Such a message was both new in the world and "good news" (gospel) for the people in the Roman world. To people in the Jesus movement, it was compelling.

To put Jesus' (and his God's) ethical ideals into practice to mutual benefit in a community was not easy, but it also was not entirely impossible. Some called it participating in "his spirit" (and, by inference, God's spirit, or the Holy Spirit), and found "his presence" (and, by inference, God's presence) with them (the Greek word for presence implies "...pitching one's tent in their midst" when they did this.) When it happened, they felt that a transformation had occurred within them, and they could see transformations in others as well. Exhilaration from such transformations, then, was also to be shared with others. These feelings were so strong that, in many if not most cases, they were translated into an additional compelling ideal to be achieved in extending the "good news" to others.

In general, such transformations form a base of relevant even if impossible ethical ideals generated from a broader concept of "love." This had never before been promulgated in history with such force in the life of a single individual. Those who lived with and "bore witness" to Jesus felt it was, indeed, a "revelation" both for what can be and what should be—the event in their histories that was understandable and made other events understandable (H. R. Niebuhr, 1941).

People in the early Jesus movement, then, were "in the world, but not of it" (cf. H. R. Niebuhr, 1951). The set of formulations they used (sometimes called "symbols" by social scientists like Harold Lasswell (1936) were certainly among the most compelling symbols ever generated in history. They were seen by many as "all things to all people," and "spoke" to many more. These symbols could become, and were, attractive to people of all stations in life from elites to slaves, whether men or women, whether Jewish or not (cf., among others, Jn 13:14). Jesus-movement people, then, felt compelled to share these symbols and experiences with others.

iv

To share experiences with people somewhat like yourself is relatively easy and the nature of the early parties within the Jesus movement underscored this. The four parties of the Jesus movement represented initial interpretations of the "meaning of Jesus" for people's lives and practices, individually and collectively, to at least four different "audiences," and largely in four different settings, but settings with which certain of Jesus' followers were familiar. The four audiences were a set of Jewish synagogues among all the synagogues in Jerusalem (visited primarily by James and the Brethren); synagogues in the region of Galilee (visited primarily by Peter and the Disciples); Hellenist Jews in Jerusalem, as well as beyond Palestine (visited by Stephen, Philip, the Beloved Disciple, and other Hellenists); and Greek-speaking gentiles, mostly in lands more distant from Palestine (by Paul and the Apostles).

Since Jesus was Jewish by birth and initially nearly all his closest followers were Jews, for them to share their experiences with other Jews came relatively easy. Accordingly, certain key followers, the Brethren in the urban setting of Jerusalem and the Disciples in the more rural settings around the Sea of Galilee, went to synagogues, settings where they felt at home and were comfortable. Such highly ethnic, somewhat provincial, focus in approach is familiar throughout history. A main theme in *The Religious Factor* by the sociologist G. E. Lenski is that people with similar ethnic (and social class) backgrounds usually hold many distinguishable beliefs in common. H. R. Niebuhr (1929) demonstrated a similar phenomenon.

But Jesus' followers also included Greek-speaking Jews. Greek-speaking synagogues, probably at least three of them, were in Jerusalem. For these followers to share their experiences with Greek speakers was an extension of the basic ethnic-social setting principle of social organization. And, as noted in previous chapters, this part of the Jesus movement included both Jews located in Jerusalem and those who lived outside Jerusalem, some from great distances such as Corinth and Rome itself.

Through these contacts, the Jesus movement was extended into parts of the world which were primarily Greek-speaking. Greek speakers, as noted previously, had different cultural backgrounds in their moral discourses when compared to Jews. Theirs was a more "philosophical" approach to life rather than one committed to a set of moral, collective, and personal Laws that the Jews believed were established by a God interested in the affairs of his "chosen" people. Multiple Greek gods played in their own theaters, which only occasionally impacted the affairs of men and women. For this part of the Jesus movement to communicate with Greek speakers effectively, especially gentiles, a new approach appropriate to the symbolism with which Greeks were familiar was necessary. The Hellenists and Apostles ignored the playful Greek gods, but they generated ways for making sense to those ethically, theoretically, and ethnically oriented in Greek society. Thus, the gospel of John opens, *En arche hen ho logos…* —"*In the beginning was the word…*" Logos (translated as "word") was largely unfamiliar to Jews as a theological concept. Jews believed that "Word" was a way that God intervened in human affairs, as *"In the beginning God created…, and God said…"* The philosophical concept of logos (roughly, a system of reasoning) was generally familiar to Greeks.

"Truth," another concept familiar in Greek culture, was identified by the Greek-speaking Jesus movement with the Greek word love (*agape,* one of three Greek words for love, the others being *philos,* brotherly love, and *eros,* sexual love). *Agape* connotes an "unconditional" love in becoming a key driving force in the world, and in this sense represented "truth." To Greek-speaking Christians, Jesus' new commandment, *"Love one another as I have loved you,"* is the driving force of the world. This formulation is found no less than nineteen times in New Testament writings (www.christnotes. org/bible).

The overall issue, then, was to make Christian symbols more compatible with symbols current in Greek culture in order to share more adequately the good news and experiences of loving with them. The ethnic-social setting principle becomes a *cultural* principle in adapting beliefs about Jesus in order to share the main principles of the Jesus movement. Much in New Testament writings focused on interpreting Jesus to audiences familiar to certain "types" of followers. The sharing was, as social scientists say, an iterative process produced in interactions between Jesus' followers and the social and cultural backgrounds of their diverse audiences.

Still, as noted in previous chapters, the variations that arose from giving different emphases to certain symbols with different audiences ultimately led to both misunderstandings and outright conflicts among the parties of the Jesus movement. The convictions underlying such contrasting emphases also threatened to tear the overall movement apart before it really got started.

V

Of the four initial parties in the Jesus movement, only the two Greek-speaking congregations ultimately survived to represent the movement beyond one generation of Jesus' crucifixion (roughly 70 C.E.). We have seen in previous chapters certain reasons for the demise of the two Jewish-centered parties within a single generation of Jesus' death, as their key leaders were killed or imprisoned. But there is also a way to characterize the lack of continuity in more general terms.

Table 5 repeats the table in the last chapter. It outlines thirteen main features of similarities and differences among the Jesus movement's four parties, most having to do with

Table 5 (repeated). Summary of the Apostles' Actions and Beliefs on Thirteen Major Issues.

Parties	The Twelve Disciples	Brethren	Hellenists	Apostles
Beginning Event	Jesus's call in Galilee	Coming of the Spirit at Pentecost	Split with Hebrew speakers and their practices	Recognized possibilities for extending the movement through missions to Gentiles
Governance	Cephas; The Twelve, the Assembly of 70	James; Elders	Seven Deacons; Philip; Beloved Disciple	Paul; Assembly of the Apostles, Barnabas
Mission Targets	Synagogues in Galilee, Gaza	Hebrew-speaking synagogues	Greek-speaking synagogues	Diaspora synagogues both Jew and Greek; God-fearers; Gentile friends
Composition of Party	Jewish men in leadership, some women	Jewish men and their families	Greek-speaking Jews, men and women	Jew, Greek; slave, free; women, men
Places of Worship	Temple, synagogues, house churches	Temple, synagogues, house churches	Synagogues, house churches	Temple, synagogues, house churches
Circumcision	Jewish men and proselytes before the Jerusalem Conference; only Jewish men after	Jewish men	Jewish men	Jewish men could be cicumcised, but Gentiles need not

Parties	The Twelve Disciples	Brethren	Hellenists	Apostles
Food Laws	Kept, then did not	Kept all kosher laws	Did or did not keep laws	Tried, but failed to keep provisions of the Conference
Marriage Laws	Married Jewish women	Married Jewish women	Married Jewish women	Marriage open to all
Theological Self-Understanding	Successor to Israel	Covenant renewed	New Israel or "Israel as originally constituted"	Those "in Christ"
Role of Jesus	Servant of God	Designated as Messiah at death, Son of David	Son of Humankind, Incarnate of God	Crucified and risen Christ
Primary Ethical Principle	"Take up cross, follow me"	"Seek God's righteousness"	"Love one another as I have loved you"	"Bear one another's burdens"
Writings	Mark 1st Peter	Matthew James Jude Revelation	John Hebrews Letters of John	Luke, Acts Romans Corinthians Galatians Ephesians Philppians colossians Thessalonians Pastorals Philemon
Terminating Event	Death of leaders under Herod Agrippa	Death of James & leaders, Jewish war 66–70 C.E.	Continued after 70 C.E.	Continued after 70 C.E.

theological-ethical formulations ("symbols") generated by the four parties as represented in their major writings. Table 5 shows considerable differentiation in the Jesus movement, resulting in conflicts among the parties that almost caused the overall movement's demise before it really established itself.

In the four parties, the main leaders were different; beginning events were different; mission targets were different; adherence to the Torah laws was different; the basic interpretation of "who Jesus was" differed in emphases; even locations for gatherings and worship differed; and the above differences contributed to differences appearing in the four parties' writings. There is variation also in *governance* among the parties.

A movement is unified both by its theological and ethical principles (its "worldview"), but also its governance. Through its governance a movement provides a means for resolving conflicts and integrating various differences into some sort of unity. In the Jesus movement, governance within the four major parties differed considerably, and one party, the Brethren, claimed, and at first received, hegemony in overall governance probably due to its more cohesive organization as well as to its claim that Jesus himself was Jewish and therefore Jewish law had to be respected.

In the two Hebrew-based parties, governance tended to focus on males and single individuals—Cephas (Peter) of the Disciples, and James of the Brethren. Both wielded considerable personal authority. Curiously, despite assertions in Matthew (16:18), Peter was not, initially at least, the rock on which the Jesus movement was to depend. Instead overall authority relatively quickly seems to have devolved to James, brother of Jesus (or was he, more accurately, the leader of the Brethren party?).

James called the Jerusalem Conference, took major leadership in it, worked out the "compromises" which favored the continuance of the food laws of the Hebrew culture of Jerusalem over the Greek speakers in the movement, and then "enforced" the compromise through his emissaries. Peter did speak eloquently at this conference (Acts 15:7–11). Still, both Peter and Paul, perhaps fearing additional violence, acceded to James's leadership. Early on, it became apparent that the Brethren party of James was willing to engage in arousing crowds to violence, and in at least one case the stoning of Stephen, in order to enforce its authority (Acts 7:59). Paul experienced such violence in many of the cities in Asia and in Greece (Acts 13:50; 14:2; 16:20–24; 17:5–9; 19:28–41; 20:1–2; especially 20:19, where Paul speaks of "the plots of the Jews"; 21:25–36; 23:12–15; 24:4–5). It seems conflicts over the outcomes of the Jerusalem compromise continued to arise between the Brethren and Jews and the Greek-speaking parties' congregations.

Unhappiness with these outcomes as well as dissent over the stoning and the "power play" of using violence (Acts 11:19) and sending two fellow Brethren from Jerusalem to accompany Paul on his journeys, for the supposed purpose of "explaining" the compromise to the Brethren living outside Palestine, as well as community disruptions in many places Paul went, gave grounds for suspicion on the part of Barnabas and Paul and their followers who believed in the Jesus movement. Besides, Paul along with Stephen and Philip seemed to have had more success with non-Jewish Greeks than with Hellenist Greeks (Acts 21:19). In any case, Paul was the focus of divisiveness among the Brethren almost everywhere he went. Despite this, Paul was convinced his convictions were valid (Acts 20:18–36; Acts 21:26), which increasingly overrode his inclinations for peacemaking that the Jesus message conveyed.

In the two Greek-speaking parties, governance and authority was apparently dispersed. Among Hellenists, authority centered around seven elders and several spokesmen, Stephen briefly and Philip longer. Governance among the Apostles was also dispersed, with much authority in the hands of individual congregations, while Paul and other Apostles became commentators on moral and conflict issues in them.

Whether Paul's suggestions were implemented, we do not know for certain. But we presume they were at least extensively discussed.

Paul's communications among the congregations, where he tried to become a moral authority to them on fundamental principles they all "should" follow, also served another, more general purpose. His letters were taken seriously enough that they were written down, undoubtedly multiple times, so that they survived his lifetime. These letters in themselves provided a unifying force among the congregations that otherwise had decentralized authority. They at least enabled the congregations to know about one another and to understand more fully the struggles of each of them. Each party also had at least one written document, "their" gospel (Matthew, Mark, John, and Luke). But, as far as we know, they had far fewer letters, communications, between their moral leaders (symbol specialists) and the congregations committed to each party.

In any case, loosely decentralized arrangements in an organization early in social movements are not unusual. Lasswell (1936) examined several developing social movements. Early in a movement "symbols specialists" (such as Stephen, Paul, Philip, Timothy, and Apollos) tend to dominate. Later, organization specialists, especially in partnership with resource specialists, tend to dominate. Occasionally, under conditions when a movement feels threatened from the outside, specialists in neutralizing violence against them tend to dominate. The balance among these four types of specialists varies with the external conditions in which organizations find themselves.

Governance in the Jesus parties also reflected cultural differences. Being unfamiliar with the concept that God "chose" a people and gave the people the law and the prophets, gentile Greeks had less reason to respond positively to ideas that grew out of a Hebrew tradition. Food laws, marriage laws, and, especially, circumcision laws made little sense to Greeks—they were not part of their cultures. But philosophy was common in almost all Greek cultures, even in those of Greek-speaking Jews. Symbols specialists took their varied cultures into account as they interpreted the significance of Jesus to followers and potential followers. Paul's speech at the Areopagus in Athens is a good example (Acts 17:16-34) where he cites various Greek cultural symbols—*"Epicureans... Stoics...[concerns with] telling or hearing something new... unknown gods...boundaries...art...imagination...[and even] ignorance."*

These symbol specialists became authoritative to Greeks by putting the significance of Jesus in philosophical terms. *"I am the way, the truth, and the life"* (Jn 14:6)—these philosophical terms were understandable to Greeks of the first century. "The Way" connotes a discipline of some sort, in general terms similar to, even if different from, the "moderation in all things" principle of Aristotle. Truth is a Greek philosophical concept from early on, but not well recognized by Jews. So, the symbol specialists that spoke Greek and went to Greek-speaking synagogues and other gentiles found common ground with them by referring to Jesus in philosophical-theological terms rather than through the more-strictly Jewish religious formulations.

Although governance per se did not appear as a self-conscious issue in the Greek-speaking congregations, when conflicts arose (an issue mostly handled through governance), symbol specialists interceded to resolve the conflicts, usually through referring to "basic" theological-ethical-philosophical issues rather than relying on Jewish or any other religious traditions for their authority. "The received wisdom" had quite different meanings to Greeks compared to Jews.

Most such conflicts in the Greek-speaking Jesus movement dealt with the significance of Jesus in people's lives, usually on whether to honor the received Jewish religious traditions of law in practice. The exclusionary acts in marriage laws, food laws, and circumcision were questioned by

Greek-speaking congregations in the Jesus movement almost from the beginning. Later, issues of authority within the congregations were also questioned. The Greek-speaking congregations tended to follow more "equal rights" principles—"... *in Christ there is no male and female, neither Jew nor Greek, neither slave nor free... We are all one in Christ*" (Gal 3:28). This contrasted with a male-dominated authority structure as in Jewish tradition and exemplified in James and Peter and almost all other Jewish figures found in the writings of the Hebrew-speakers (where, for instance, Mary Magdalene is largely excluded). After about 100 c.e., most Christian churches also tended toward male dominance, but the early Greek-speaking congregations in the Jesus movement apparently did not.

vi

The demise of Hebrew-speaking congregations in Jerusalem in the early Jesus movement before 70 c.e. is another example in which governance played a major role. Little was said about this demise in the Greek-speakers' writings (the primary ones easily accessed). References to the Hebrew-speaking parties simply stopped. In effect, those practicing exclusivity, that is, the Hebrew-speaking congregations by their adherence to Jewish traditions, were themselves excluded by other Jews. They were read out of their synagogues, declared "dead" to other religious Jews, and lost the "community" provided by Jerusalem's large Jewish population. As we saw in previous chapters, this loss of community by Hebrew-speaking Jews in the Jesus movement removed them from their traditional livelihoods. They sent word of their needs for money to congregations throughout the diaspora, and many outlying congregations responded by remitting funds. Paul, among others, brought some of these funds when he visited Jerusalem (Acts 11:29).

But apparently James and other leaders in the Hebrew-speaking Jesus movement, feeling their commitments deeply, kept up their preaching challenging the ideas of those in traditional Jewish synagogues, and many were finally executed for their Jesus-based "apostate" efforts. No new leadership developed after James was executed and Peter exiled. For all intents and purposes, the Jesus movement died in Jerusalem and Palestine, and/or was, in effect, either neutralized or exiled to other parts of the known world seldom heard from again as a major force in the Jesus movement. Hebrew-speaking congregations in the Jesus movement lost their hegemony.

Such scenarios can also be considered a product of a lack of a self-consciously viable form of governance. Specifically, Hebrew-speaking congregations in Jerusalem failed to provide for livelihoods for their congregants, or for a continuing leadership when current leaders might become unavailable for any reason. The movement died when the original leaders died. Max Weber would have called this a failure to "routinize charisma," that is, a failure to provide continuity for leadership in the movement when a given leader was removed.

Many social movements in history have died under this scenario, such as John the Baptist's movement, the Qumran community, slave uprisings, and even early "Protest-ant" movements in the late Middle Ages such as the one led by John Hus. Most Utopian movements died when the original leadership died. In contrast, events among the Mormons when Joseph Smith was killed enabled a new and stronger leadership to emerge under Brigham Young. Still, the principle, "Cut off the head of the leader and the movement dies," has strong support in history.

The failure to provide such continuity in leadership greatly reduces the ability of a movement to adapt, accommodate, or remain flexible and viable in the face of outside threats. Exclusionary groups with "boundaries" not easily penetrated by outside forces are particularly vulnerable, whether the movement is utopian or terrorist. Social scientists call this practice the open-closed dimension. "Open" movements are generally more likely to adapt (*"...give unto Caesar that which is Caesar's...,"* Mt 22:21; Mk 12:17, Lk 20:25), perhaps changing their characters somewhat in the process (called, in social science, "adaptive strategies"), while "closed" (exclusionary) movements, like the Qumran community, are more likely to disappear entirely.

Open social movements are also more likely to have more flexible internal communication networks (called "internal fluidity of information and resources") which permit new ideas about continuity and viability to come forth for consideration and eventual resolution. In contrast to Hebrew-speaking Jesus-movement congregations in the Roman Empire, Paul's and the other Apostles' Greek-speaking congregations, with their greater equality among members, along with Paul's letter-writing communications making them aware of the more-inclusive movement of which they were a part, apparently gave these congregations greater capabilities for survival. Such differences permitted Greek-speaking congregations in the Jesus movement to prosper relative to the Hebrew-speaking congregations, which comparatively quickly faded into history—within one generation of the loss of its original charismatic leader, Jesus and then James (and many other of the Brethren and Disciples).

Paul's letter-writing communications gave the Greek-speaking congregations another advantage. In *The Tipping Point*, Malcolm Gladwell built on the work of the sociologist Mark Granovetter (1973) by using the concept of "the strength of weak ties." Paul might well have been the tipping point in giving these congregations unity and strength through "weakly" relating them to one another. At least, he was part of many churches, and documented both the churches and their problems—among others, Romans, Corinthians, Galatians, Ephesians, Philippians, and Thessalonians. In other words, he was well-known in these cities, wrote about issues they faced, and, apparently, his works were shared among the churches. One reason Peter or the Brethren might have been less "successful" than Paul in their evangelizing was that they wrote less (if anything). Even if "history is written by the victors," and Paul, Luke, and other Apostles ended up being part of the victors in the church, the ties represented major linkages among the churches, which contributed to their "strength" in a relatively "open" set of social organizations. But, of course, this also is hindsight.

vii

Although the "love" theme is found in all the gospels, the explicit formulation of "love one another" is found primarily among the Greek-speaking congregations in the Jesus movement. Both the gospel of John, attributed to the Hellenists, and the Apostle Paul in his various letters emphasized this theme.

Such a formulation can be related to another key principle among social scientists, the so-called "warm-cold variable." People tend to respond positively to others they deem "warm," and less positively, or even negatively, to those they deem "cold." In contemporary society, a major difference between African-American churches and Caucasian churches, according to many African-Americans, is that Caucasian churches are "cold" while African-American churches are "warm."

The "love one another" formulation as a central theme in the Greek-speaking movement can be recognized as a "warm" principle. The "warm" principle is found in the gospel of John, and Paul's letters to the Romans, Galatians, Ephesians, Thessalonians, as well as in the Letter to the Hebrews and epistles of John. The closest to this formulation in the Hebrew-speaking writings is "love thy neighbor as thyself" (Mt 5:43, 19:19, 22:39; Mk 12:31; Lk 10:27; James 2:8). It is drawn from the Jewish law-book of Leviticus (19:18). A version of "love one another" is also found in 1 Peter 1:22, which has been attributed to Mark.

The warmth of caring shown in "love one another" along with "equality" ("neither slave nor free...") and "openness" in their practices (optional food, marriage, and circumcision laws), among Greek-speaking congregations also gave them flexibility, adaptability, and vitality in their ethical and theological priorities found less often in the Hebrew-speaking congregations. To Greek speakers, the God of love was in their midst through the love one member had for another. As Rodney Stark (1996) asserts, these advantages accounted in large part for their continuance and viability in their missions to extend the principles of the Jesus movement to others in the far reaches of the Roman Empire by the year 70 C.E.

viii

The historical period from Paul in Rome, and thereafter to about 100 C.E., remains covered in controversy. But most commentaries indicate some sort of self-conscious organization among the congregations of the Jesus movement (at least by 100 C.E.). Or, perhaps the churches in Rome sent out emissaries in helping to organize the more distant churches into a confederation where the Roman church had hegemony. Still, little doubt remains that what was to become both the Roman Catholic Church and Eastern Orthodox Church had roots in the previous period and thus the movement evolved into the world's oldest continuous bureaucracy (Collins, 1980).

In any case, from a series of mostly decentralized congregations, unorganized in relation to one another, the Christian movement became self-consciously organized. It might have done so simply so that, as with the Jews, it could have a semi-autonomous, *politeuma* in the Roman cities. The Jews had their own councils, their own courts, and their own religious practices, which had their origins relatively deep in Roman history. Christians undoubtedly desired such recognition, and therefore they felt a need to organize adequately in order to attain this status in Roman society.

The step to organization, as H. D. Lasswell (1936) and Max Weber (1947) noted, was crucial for the long-term survival of any movement, including the Christian movement. Once the churches became relatively centrally organized, with moderate flexibility to respond to local conditions, no longer could Roman pogroms against Christians go without organized repercussions when they occurred. Some authorities were probably chided when they attempted to impose universal sacrifices to the Emperor. Even though many Christians were martyred, the numbers remain vague, and certainly not all Roman Emperors engaged in systematic persecution practices throughout the Empire. The organization among the Christian congregations into a confederation, now officially called churches, contributed to the comparative ineffectiveness of "official" sacrificial rites to the Emperor. This organization also generated resources through "resource specialists" and countered threats through "threats specialists" (to use Lasswell's concepts).

But movement to a better organized church also shifted major leadership in the churches from "symbol specialists" like Paul to "organization specialists" like the Bishops of Rome, Antioch, Alexandria, and Jerusalem. Some, like Augustine of Hippo (354–430 C.E.), were examples of being both symbols specialists and organization specialists. Finally, however, a Pope appeared to have aggregated much authority, temporal through its organization and moral in establishing doctrinal rules for all in the Church to follow, all the while accumulating a good deal of wealth and influence.

Organization also implies that resources to support the structure were to be found, and threats, especially physical threats to it, to be neutralized. Thus, as in many social movements, a pluralism of leadership developed – the symbol specialists continued, but cooperated with (even if occasionally competing against) "resource specialists" and "threats specialists" (Lasswell, 1936). Lasswell tells us that, in the Nazi movement, for instance, Goebbels was the symbol specialist, Goering a resource specialist, and Himmler (of the SS) the threats specialist, with Hitler as a symbol specialist at the beginning of the movement but becoming an organization specialist when the movement became legitimated. Goebbels, we are told, was angry at his comparative downgrading once the Nazi movement attained political legitimacy.

Similar specialists, with some competition among different specialists, can be found within the Christian churches at various points in their history. When such specialists do not appear, social analysts imply, social movements do not survive. Martin Luther was an example of a teacher who became a "competitor" symbol specialist by challenging certain "resource specialists" in the Roman Catholic Church. Luther, on issues of indulgences and the resources these brought to the Church, challenged the Catholic Church's resource specialists by pounding his 95 theses on the door of the church in Wittenberg in 1517. But it also took the organization (and threats) specialists of local (partially "secular") political elites to initially protect him and his movement and deflect threats made on him.

But this goes well beyond the 70 C.E. of our present study, and historians have many treatises on later developments in Christianity. The roots of these later historical periods, however, were in place in the first generation of the Jesus movement. Greek-speaking theological and ethical principles survived and thus dominated and spread. As in the early parts of most social movements, symbol specialists were predominant in determining the principles people relied on in their congregations and gave a missionary zeal for spreading the gospel (the "good news") about the power of Jesus' love and caring in transforming ordinary and extraordinary lives. Perhaps all this becomes more understandable to some because they saw it happening in their own lives and among their fellow beings. This was the process that Weber identified as being necessary to the health and growth of an organization that became ever more hierarchical and bureaucratic. The "charisma" of Jesus started to become "routinized," largely through Paul and the congregations with which he was identified.

ix

In 1956, H. R. Niebuhr, Williams, and Gustafson published their book, *The Purpose of the Church and Its Ministry.* Early in the book they reviewed the varieties of formulations used in guiding this purpose. At the end of the review they ask the question, "Is not the end of these formulations summarized in this one statement, to increase among men (sic) the love of God and neighbor?" They then go on to explain the words, "love" (joy, gratitude, respect, and loyalty) and "neighbor" (all people).

Their particular formulation for the church's purpose, "increase of love among neighbors," stands as a challenge to church leaders and social scientists. How do we evaluate this? We noted earlier that the parties of the Jesus movement that had the most success in ministry were those that conducted ministries that were inclusive, and that might be our clue. How inclusive are today's church families? Each faces challenges as demanding as those faced by the original parties in the Jesus movement.

We can list some of these challenges. Internal to a society, they have to do with the manner in which the churches respond to issues of race, gender, and sexual orientation. External to a society, issues include poverty, ecology, and war. Evaluations should be made on the official statements of each church family or, lacking such statements, its prevalent practices. Definitions of the issues include the following:

On poverty: Does the church encourage charity alone *and* move beyond that to deal with the systemic issues that cause poverty?

On ecology: Does it officially encourage persons both to take individual steps to help to eliminate global warming and other ecological issues—the health of flora and fauna—*and* actively work for policies to achieve the increase of health upon the planet?

On war: Does the church both mobilize itself to fight any war determined by the governing bodies of the nation *and* maintain a critical standard on the matter of war, such as supporting no war or any "just and mournful war"?

On internal issues:

Race: Is membership open to all persons regardless of race?

Gender: Are leadership positions in the church, including ordination to church office, open to all persons who are members of the church?

Sexual orientation: Is membership in the church open to all regardless of sexual orientation? Is leadership in the church open to all?

By placing these on a grid in a heuristic Table 6, each reader can make her or his judgment as to whether each church family has fulfilled Niebuhr's criteria of working for the increase in the world of love of God and neighbor.

Table 6. Key Issues Facing Christian Churches in the 21st Century.

Issue	Eastern Orthodox	Roman Catholic	Evangelical	"Mainline" Protestant	African-American
External to a Society or a Church					
Poverty					
Ecology					
War					
Internal to a Society or a Church					
Race					
Gender					
Sexual Orientation					

Rodney Stark (1996: 160–161) describes what the first generations of Christians meant to the world. "To cities filled with hopeless and impoverished people, Christianity offered charity as well as hope. To cities filled with newcomers and strangers, Christianity offered an immediate basis for attachments. To cities filled with orphans and widows, Christianity provided a new and expanded sense of family. To cities faced with epidemics, fires and earthquakes, Christianity offered effective nursing services. To cities torn by violent ethnic strife, Christianity offered a new basis for social solidarity…. Christianity revitalized life in Greco-Roman cities by providing new norms and new kinds of social relationships able to cope with urgent urban problems" (slightly re-arranged from the original). These early Christians put Jesus Christ at the center of their lives. Through their communities they reached out to include all kinds of persons into their fellowships. These sentences end Stark's book: "Christians effectively promulgated a moral vision utterly incompatible with the casual cruelty of pagan custom. What Christianity gave its converts was nothing less than their humanity" (215).

This is the paradigm for working to increase in the world the love of God and neighbor. All our contemporary churches, successors to the parties of the Jesus movement, should be engaged in nothing less.

Bibliography

Abrahamsen, Valerie A., 1988. *Biblical Archaeology,* 51 (1), 46–56.

Agnew, F., 1986. "The Origin of the New Testament Apostle-Concept: A Review of Research," *Journal of Biblical Literature*, 105, 1: 75–96.

Balsdon, J. P. V. D., 1998. *Roman Women: Their History and Habits.* New York: Barnes and Noble Books.

Bammel, Ernst (editor), 1970. *The Trial of Jesus: Cambridge Studies in Honour of C. F. D. Moule.* London: SCM Press.

Barrett, C. K. , 1967. *Jesus and the Gospel Tradition.* London: S.P.C.K.

Bellah, Robert, et al., 1985. *Habits of the Heart.* Berkeley, Los Angeles, London: University of California Press.

Blasi, Anthony J., 1995. "Office Charisma in Early Christian Ephesus," *Sociology of Religion,* 56: 245–256.

Blasi, Anthony J., 1996. *A Sociology of Johannine Christianity.* Lewiston, N.Y.: The Edward Mellen Press.

Bowman, Alan K., 1986. *Egypt after the Pharaohs.* Berkeley: The University of California Press, 209.

Brandon, S. G. F., 1967. *Jesus and the Zealots.* New York: Charles Scribner's Sons, 300, 306.

Brandon, S. G. F., 1967. *The Trial of Jesus of Nazareth.* New York: Stein and Day.

Brown, R. E., 1966. *The Gospel according to John.* Garden City, N.Y.: Doubleday & Company, Chapters 1–12.

Brown, R. E. , 1970. *The Gospel according to John.* Garden City, N.Y.: Doubleday & Company, Chapters 13–21.

Brown, R. E., 1979. *The Community of the Beloved Disciple.* New York, Toronto: Ramsey/Paulist Press.

Brown, R. E., 1983. "Not Jewish Christianity and Gentile Christianity but Types of Jewish/Gentile Christianity," *Catholic Biblical Quarterly,* 83, 1: 74–79.

Brown, R. E., with J. P Meier, 1983. *Antioch and Rome.* New York: Ramsey/Paulist Press.

Bruce, F. F., 1979. *Peter, Stephen, James, and John.* Grand Rapids, Mich.: Eerdmanns.

Brueggemann, Walter, 1999. *The Christian Century.* March 24–31, p. 345.

Cohen, Shaye J. D., 1987. *From the Maccabees to the Mishnah.* Philadelphia: Westminster Press, 109.

Collins, Randall, 1980. "Weber's Last Theory of Capitalism: A Systematization." *American Sociological Review,* 45 (December): 925–942.

Conzelmann, Hans, 1973. *History of Primitive Christianity.* New York, Nashville: Abingdon.

Cullmann, Oscar, 1953. *Peter: Disciple, Apostle, Martyr.* London: SCM Press.

Cullmann, Oscar, 1976. *The Johannine Circle.* Philadelphia: Westminster Press.

Culpepper, R. A., 1975. *The Johannine School.* Missoula, Mont.: Scholars Press.

Davies, W. D., 1962. *Christian Origins and Judaism.* Philadelphia: The Westminster Press.

deCamp, L. Sprague, 1972. *Great Cities of the Ancient World.* Garden City, N.Y.: Doubleday.

Dodd, C. H., 1954. *The Interpretation of the Fourth Gospel.* Cambridge, U.K.: Cambridge University Press, 54–73.

Dodd, C. H. , 1963. *Historical Tradition in the Fourth Gospel.* Cambridge, U.K.: Cambridge University Press.

Eberts, Harry W., Jr., 1987. *We Believe: A Study of the Book of Confessions for Church Officers.* Philadelphia: Geneva Press.

Eberts, Harry W., Jr., 1997. "Plurality and Ethnicity in Early Christian Mission," *Sociology of Religion,* 58, 4 (Winter), 305–321.

Eberts, Paul R., 2004. *Well-Being Indicators for New York State,*

1950–2000. Albany, N.Y.: Legislation Commission on Rural Resources.

Eisenman, Robert, 1997. *James, the Brother of Jesus.* New York: Penguin Books.

Ellens, J. Harold, 1997. "The Ancient Library of Alexandria: The West's Most important Repository of Learning," *Bible Review,* XIII, (1), 18ff.

Elliott-Binns, L. E., 1956. *Galilean Christianity.* Longbank Works, Alva: Robert Cunningham and Sons, Ltd.

Erdemgil, Selahattin, 1989. *Ephesus, Ruins and Museum.* Istanbul: Net Turistik Yayinlar A. S.

Eusebius Pamphilius, Bishop of Caesarea, 4th Century C.E. *The Ecclesiastical History.* Translated by Cruse, C. F. (1879). London: George Bell and Sons.

Ferguson, Everett, 1993. *Backgrounds of Early Christianity.* Grand Rapids, Mich.: Eerdmanns. Second Edition, 32.

Filson, Floyd, 1950. *The New Testament Against Its Environment.* London: SCM Press Ltd.

Finley, M. I., 1980. *Ancient Slavery and Modern Ideology.* New York: The Viking Press.

Finley, M. I., 1985. *Ancient History.* London: George Bell. New York: The Viking Press.

Fiorenza, Elisabeth Schussler, 1983. *In Memory of Her: A Feminist Theological Reconstruction of Christian Origins.* New York: Crossroads.

Frend, W. H. C., 1967. *Martyrdom and Persecution in the Early Church.* Garden City, N.Y.: Anchor Books, Doubleday & Company, 97.

Gladwell, Malcolm (2000). *The Tipping Point: How Little Things Can Make a Big Difference.* New York: Little, Brown.

Granovetter, Mark S. (1973). "The Strength of Weak Ties," *American Journal of Sociology,* 78, 6, 1360 ff.

Grant, Michael, 1973. *The Jews in the Roman World.* (No city listed): Dorset Press. 58-59, 133–136, 191–192.

Grant, Michael, 1975. *The Twelve Caesars.* New York: Charles Scribner's Sons.

Grant, Michael, 1978. *History of Rome.* New York: Charles Scribner's Sons.

Grant, Robert M., 1970. *Augustus to Constantine.* San Francisco: Harper and Row.

Gruen, Erich S., 1998. *Heritage and Hellenism.* Berkeley, Los Angeles, and London: University of California Press.

Hadas-Lebel, Mireille, 1993. *Flavius Josephus: Eyewitness to Rome's First-Century Conquest of Judea.* New York: Macmillan Publishing Company.

Harnack, Adolph von, 1909. *The Acts of the Apostles.* London: Williams & Norgate.

Harris, William, 1982. "Sounding Brass and Hellenistic Technology." *Biblical Archaeological Reader,* 8, 1: 38–41.

Hayes, Richard B., 1996. *The Moral Vision of the New Testament: Community, Cross, New Creation.* New York: HarperCollins Publishers.

Hengel, Martin, 1989. *The 'Hellenization' of Judaea in the First Century After Christ.* Philadelphia: Trinity Press International.

Hock, Ronald F., 1980. *The Social Context of Paul's Ministry: Tentmaking and Apostleship.* Philadelphia: Fortress Press.

Horsley, Richard A., with J. S. Hanson, 1985. *Bandits, Prophets, and Messiahs: Popular Movements at the Time of Jesus.* San Francisco: Harper and Row.

Horsley, Richard A., 1989. *Sociology and the Jesus Movement.* New York: Crossroads.

Horsley, Richard A., 1996. *Archaeology, History and Society in Galilee: The Social Context of Jesus and the Rabbis.* Valley Forge, Penna.: Trinity Press International, 146–148.

In Flaccum, 85, recounted in A. K. Bowman, 1986: 216.

Iris Habib el Masri, 1956. *The Story of the Copts.* [No city given]: Middle East Council of Churches, "In Egypt we beheld (Christ's) glory since 61 C.E., when St. Mark came to proclaim the Gospel in obedience to the Holy Spirit," 13. A footnote reads: "This is the date recorded in the Coptic Annals; other historians say that it was about the year 55 C.E.," 17.

Jacobs, Jane, 1961. *Death and Life of Great American Cities.* New York: Random House.

Jacobs, Jane, 1969. *The Economy of Cities.* New York: Random House.

Johnson, Sherman E., 1987. *Paul, the Apostle and His Cities.* Wilmington, Del.: Michael Glazier.

Jones, A. H. M., 1940. *The Greek City.* New York: Oxford University Press.

Josephus, Flavius. (no date). *Wars of the Jews.* Book VII, Chapter X, Philadelphia: Porter and Coates, 855

Kamil, Jill, 1987. *Coptic Egypt.* Cairo: The American University in Cairo Press.

Kee, Howard C., 1977. *Community of the New Age: Studies in Mark's Gospel.* Philadelphia: Westminster Press

Kee, Howard C., 1995. *Who Are the People of God? Early Christian Models of Community.* New Haven, Conn., and London: Yale University Press.

Kee, Howard C., 1997. *To Every Nation Under Heaven: The Acts of the Apostles.* Harrisburg, Penna.: Trinity Press International.

Kelley, Harold H., 1950. "The Warm-Cold Variable in First Impressions of People," *Journal of Personality,* 18, 4:431–439.

Knohl, Israel, 2008. "The Messiah: Son of Joseph—'Gabriel Revelation' and the Birth of a New Messianic Model," *Biblical Archaeology Review,* 34, 5 (Nov./Dec.), 58–62.

Lasswell, Harold D., 1936. *Politics: Who Gets What, When, How.* New York: McGraw-Hill (also 1950, 1958).

Lenski, Gerhard E., 1961. *The Religious Factor.* New York: Doubleday.

Levick, Barbara, 1990. *Claudius.* New Haven, Conn.: Yale University Press.

Lightfoot, Joseph B., 1865. *Saint Paul's Letter to the Galatians.* London: Macmillan.

Lohse, Eduard, 1976. *The New Testament Environment.* Nashville: Abingdon.

Longenecker, Richard N., 1970. *The Christology of Early Jewish Christianity.* London: SCM Press Ltd.

Malina, Bruce J., 1993. *The New Testament World: Insights from Cultural Anthropology.* Louisville, Ky.: Westminster/ John Knox Press.

Manson, T. W., 1963. *On Paul and John.* London: SCM Press Ltd.

Meeks, Wayne A., 1983. *The First Urban Christians.* New Haven, Conn. and London: Yale University Press.

Meeks, Wayne A., 1986. *The Moral World of the First Christians.* Philadelphia: The Westminster Press.

Meinardus, Otto F. A., 1986. *The Holy Family in Egypt.* Cairo: The American University in Cairo Press.

Meinardus, Otto F. A., 1989. *St. Paul in Greece.* Athens: Lycabettus Press, 5th edition.

Mendels, Doron, 1992. *The Rise and Fall of Jewish Nationalism: Jewish and Christian Ethnicity in Ancient Palestine.* New York: Doubleday.

Meyer, B. F., 1986. *The Earliest Christians: Their World Mission and Self-Discovery.* Wilmington, Del.: Michael Glazier.

Murphy-O'Conner, Jerome, 1999. "Fishers of Fish, Fishers of Men," *Bible Review,* 15, 3: 23–28, 48.

Mulholland, J. Robert, Jr., 1981. "The Infancy Narrative in Matthew and Luke—Of History, Theology, and Liberation (a review of R. E. Brown's *Birth of the Messiah*)," quoting Brown, R. E., *Biblical Archaeological Review,* 7, 2 (Mar/Apr.): 53.

Neusner, Jacob, 1973. *From Politics to Piety.* Englewood Cliffs, N.J.: Prentice-Hall, Inc., 98.

Neusner, Jacob, 1975. *First Century Judaism in Crisis.* Nashville and New York: Abingdon, 183.

Neusner, Jacob, 1984. *Judaism in the Beginning of Christianity.* Philadelphia: Fortress Press.

New Testament, The:
   The Gospel of Matthew
   The Gospel of Mark
   The Gospel of Luke
   The Gospel of John
   The Acts of the Apostles
   Paul's Letter to the Romans

Paul's Letter to the Ephesians
Paul's Letters to the Corinthians
Paul's Letter to the Galatians
Paul's Letter to the Philippians
The Letter to the Hebrews
The Letters of John
The Revelation of John

Newbigin, Lesslie, 1986. *Foolishness to the Greeks, The Gospel and Western Culture.* Grand Rapids, Mich.: Eerdmanns.

Newsweek, 2008. Ron Chusid, "Tolerance for gays to marry," December 6.

Nickle, Keith F., 1966. *The Collection.* London: SCM Press Ltd.

Niebuhr, H. Richard, 1954 (orig. 1929). *Social Sources of Denominationalism.* Hamden, Conn.: Shoe String Press.

Niebuhr, H. Richard, 1941. *The Meaning of Revelation.* New York: Macmillan Company.

Niebuhr, H. Richard, 1951. *Christ and Culture.* New York: Harper.

Niebuhr, H. Richard, Daniel Day Williams, and James Gustafson, 1956. *The Purpose of the Church and Its Ministries.* New York: Harper and Row.

Niebuhr, Reinhold, 1935. *An Interpretation of Christian Ethics: The Relevance of an Impossible Ethical Ideal.* New York: Charles Scribner's Sons.

Osiek, Carolyn, 1992. *What Are They Saying about the Social Setting of the New Testament?* New York/Mahwah, N.J.: Paulist Press.

Papahatzis, Nicos, 1985. *Ancient Corinth.* Athens: Ekdotike Athenon S. A.

Pratsidou, Alexandra, 1989. *Saint Paul in Philippi.* (No city given): Tzivanakis Press.

Richardson, Peter, 1996. *Herod: King of the Jews and Friend of the Romans.* Columbia: University of South Carolina Press.

Rhoads, David M., 1976. *Israel in Revolution, 6–74 c.e.* Philadelphia: Fortress Press.

Richardson, Cyril C., editor, 1953. "The Didache," *Vol One: Early Christian Fathers. Library of Christians Classics.* Philadelphia: The Westminster Press.

Sandmel, Samuel, 1979. *Philo of Alexandria, An Introduction.* New York and Oxford: Oxford University Press, 160–161

Schmithals, Walter, 1965. *James and Paul.* London: SCM Press.

Schmithals, Walter, 1969. *The Office of Apostle in the Early Church.* New York and Nashville: Abingdon.

Schonfield, Hugh J., 1965. *The Passover Plot: New Light on the History of Jesus.* New York: Random House.

Stambaugh, J. E., and Balch, D. L., 1986. *The New Testament in Its Social Environment.* Philadelphia: Westminster Press.

Stark, Rodney, 1996. *The Rise of Christianity.* Princeton, N.J.: The Princeton University Press.

Stendahl, Krister, 1968. *The School of St. Matthew.* Philadelphia: Fortress Press.

Temme, J. M., 1991. "The Shepherds' Role," *Bible Today,* 29, 6: 376–378.

Terrien, Samuel, 1985. *Till the Heart Sings: A Biblical Theology of Manhood and Womanhood.* Philadelphia: Fortress Press, 146–153.

Thiessen, Gerd, 1977. *Sociology of Early Palestinian Christianity.* Philadelphia: Fortress Press.

Warden, Duane and Roger S. Bagnall, 1988. "The Forty Thousand Citizens of Ephesus," *Classical Philology,* 83, 3: 220–223.

Weber, Maximillan, 1947 (orig. 1922). *Theory of Social and Economic Organization.* Chapter: "The Nature of Charismatic Authority and its Routinization," translated by A. R. Anderson and Talcott Parsons.

Wuellner, Wilhelm H., 1967. *The Meaning of "Fishers of Men."* Philadelphia: The Westminster Press.

Suggested Further Readings

We believe our work is largely based on our original studies of the New Testament books. If our ideas had been previously discovered and written down, there would have been no reason for us to write.

As an instance (among several), our work on Paul is based on a rather unconventional reading of his letters—an understanding that we believe is correct, of course. In our work, we have tried to put the letters in the historical order in which they were written for finding similarities and differences. His first letter was Galatians, where he set out his position as he wanted it to be. Then came the Jerusalem conference, which forced certain changes on him that he tried, with some misgivings, to uphold; ultimately he found that he could not. Then came First Thessalonians (which, in our judgment, added little to his overall thinking and is thus omitted here for the sake of brevity). Then came the important letters to the Corinthians, which showed how the compromises and edicts coming from the Jerusalem Conference could not hold in a Gentile world. His next letter was to the Romans; in it, despite certain misgivings, he urges his followers to accept the Jewish-Christian leadership that returned there following the death of Claudius. Then, finally, came the letter to the Philippians showing how Paul changed as he faced the new (to him) world of gentiles who became Christian but who did not have, know, or understand the Jewish experience.

All this is original in our studies and our thinking; it is the reason that even Barth's understanding of Romans differs from ours. Barth tried to theologize this letter, but in our view it was less a theological and more an apologetic book. We also believe Gary Wills assumed that Paul was the same at the end as he was at the beginning. But our readings of Paul show that he shifted considerably as he faced different situations nearly every place he went, and that he tried to stay the same, but realized he could not.

As another instance, we have taken seriously what Luke said at the beginning of the Acts—that he wasn't a creative writer but was instead putting together what had come to him. Harnack provided some documentary support for this theory, but did not take his documentation to the extent of showing that different Christian parties produced the materials. Having materials either in written or oral form that comes from each of the four parties, Luke pasted them together as best he could with very little comment. Following up on Luke's lead was very important to us, even if no previous writer to our knowledge seriously took Luke at his word to put him in the context of four sometimes competing, sometimes cooperating "parties" (a term used several times in Paul's letters).

A third instance was our use of quoted creeds and confessions of the earliest churches, especially those developed by the Brethren that Paul uses so frequently. We do not find these in current writing about the New Testament. But if we don't take them seriously, we believe Paul is misunderstood in his thinking and we learn little about the Brethren since their writing, if there was any, has not been found except as we noted (the Gospel of Matthew, James, Jude, and Revelations).

A final instance builds on the deep historical sense that these earliest Christians had—they list the resurrection appearances, whatever they were, in the order that they occurred, but with a shift in order given by those Paul met in Jerusalem, Peter and James, indicative of shifts in power in the church.

In any case, it is due to what we believe is the originality of our work that it is hard to pinpoint books to which a reader might turn in finding details about our writing. We believe we have produced fundamentally creative scholarship that does not depend directly on others' works—though certainly some illuminate what we have done. Schmithals' work on the Apostles, noted in the bibliography, comes closest to our thinking. We realize all this seems rather arrogant on our part but we also believe our work about the earliest Jesus parties comes closer than other contemporary writers to what actually happened then.

The following list, then follows from these premises, and comprises good, interesting, provocative, and eminently worthwhile books—but are not definitive for our work.

Bainton, Roland, 1950. *Here I Stand: A Life of Martin Luther.* Nashville: Abingdon. This is an eminently readable study of the interplay of life and times of the revolutionary who led the Protestant reformation. As readable a book on the other main revolutionary, John Calvin, has not yet been written, but several worthy attempts have been made. See McGrath, Alister E., 1990. *A Life of John Calvin,* Oxford: Basil Blackwell, which we think catches Calvin better than Parker, T.H.L., 2006, *John Calvin: A Biography.* Oxford: Lion Hudson plc.

Borg, Marcus J., 2006, *Jesus.* New York: HarperCollins, especially pp. 77–164. This book provides an excellent account of Jesus against the context of his world.

Bruce, F. F., 1979. *Peter, Stephen, James, and John.* Grand Rapids, MI: Eerdmanns (seminal in thinking about these men).

Frank, Harry Thomas, 1975. *Discovering the Biblical World.* Maplewood, NJ: Hammond Incorporated. This book, while older than most on this list, still provides an important look at the biblical world from its beginning to the end of the New Testament period. Keep in mind when reading this book that there are five stages of development of Scripture: Most Important Persons; Agreed-upon Dates;

Social Movements within Scripture; Writing It Down; Accepting a Canon.

Neusner, Jacob, 1973. *From Politics to Piety*. Englewood Cliffs, NJ: Prentice-Hall, Inc. An important book on the hows and whys of the Pharisees changing their political views to ones of personal piety—is the reverse true among some Christians in contemporary society? This is the best study of Phariseeism that we have found.

Newbigin, J.E. Lesslie, 1986. *Foolishness to the Greeks: The Gospel and Western Culture*. Grand Rapids, MI: Eerdmanns. This is a groundbreaking work on the interplay between Christianity and the contemporary world.

Niebuhr, H. Richard, Daniel Day Williams, and James Gustafson, 1956. *The Purpose of the Church and its Ministries*. New York: Harper and Row. This book is "deep background" to the four parties of our study, the context from which we wrote the present document.

Niebuhr, Reinhold, 1935. *An Interpretation of Christian Ethics: The Relevance of an Impossible Ethical Ideal*. New York: Charles Scribner's Sons. This book is dated but still relevant, another "deep background" book. Reinhold Niebuhr's books (he is Richard's older brother) were enormously influential in this field in the mid-20th century, although except for this one, we personally found Richard's books to be more readable—of course Richard was a professor to both of us at Yale Divinity School and this probably reflects our bias, as well.

Richardson, Peter. 1996. *Herod, King of the Jews and Friend of the Romans*. Columbia: University of South Carolina Press. A marvelous historical study, it provides insight into the world we are dealing with.

Rhoads, David. M. 1976. *Israel in Revolution, 6–74 C.E.* Philadelphia: Fortress Press. A readable overview of this important set of events in history.

Stark, Rodney. 1996. *The Rise of Christianity*. Princeton, NJ: Princeton University Press A hugely influential book on our thinking and work.

Wills, Garry, 2006. *What Paul Meant*. New York: Viking. An eminently readable book that elucidates Paul's influence on Christianity, but which gives only minimal recognition to Paul's struggles with different interpretations by other significant figures in the Jesus movement.

CPSIA information can be obtained at www.ICGtesting.com
Printed in the USA
BVOW04s0548270913

332258BV00001B/37/P